Take Your Life Back

TAKE YOUR LIFE BACK

How to Stop Letting the Past
and Other People Control You

STEPHEN ARTERBURN, M.Ed.
DAVID STOOP, Ph.D.

TYNDALE
MOMENTUM™

*The nonfiction imprint of
Tyndale House Publishers, Inc.*

Visit Tyndale online at www.tyndale.com.

Visit Tyndale Momentum online at www.tyndalemomentum.com.

TYNDALE, Tyndale Momentum, and Tyndale's quill logo are registered trademarks of Tyndale House Publishers, Inc. The Tyndale Momentum logo is a trademark of Tyndale House Publishers, Inc. Tyndale Momentum is the nonfiction imprint of Tyndale House Publishers, Inc., Carol Stream, Illinois.

Take Your Life Back: How to Stop Letting the Past and Other People Control You

Designed by Ron Kaufmann

The authors are represented by the literary agency of WordServe Literary Group, www.wordserveliterary.com.

Unless otherwise indicated, all Scripture quotations are taken from the *Holy Bible*, New Living Translation, copyright © 1996, 2004, 2015 by Tyndale House Foundation. Used by permission of Tyndale House Publishers, Inc., Carol Stream, Illinois 60188. All rights reserved.

Scripture quotations marked NIV are taken from the Holy Bible, *New International Version,*® NIV.® Copyright © 1973, 1978, 1984, 2011 by Biblica, Inc.® Used by permission. All rights reserved worldwide.

Scripture quotations marked TLB are taken from *The Living Bible*, copyright © 1971 by Tyndale House Foundation. Used by permission of Tyndale House Publishers, Inc., Carol Stream, Illinois 60188. All rights reserved.

For information about special discounts for bulk purchases, please contact Tyndale House Publishers at csresponse@tyndale.com or call 800-323-9400.

Library of Congress Cataloging-in-Publication Data
Names: Arterburn, Stephen, date, author. | Stoop, David A., author.
Title: Take your life back : how to stop letting the past and other people
    control you / Stephen Arterburn, M.Ed., David Stoop, Ph.D.
Description: Carol Stream, IL : Tyndale House Publishers, Inc., 2016. |
    Includes bibliographical references.
Identifiers: LCCN 2016023300| ISBN 9781496417817 (hc) | ISBN 9781496413673 (sc)
Subjects: LCSH: Self-actualization (Psychology—Religious
    aspects—Christianity. | Interpersonal relations—Religious
    aspects—Christianity. | Regret—Religious aspects—Christianity. | Change
    (Psychology—Religious aspects—Christianity. | Shame—Religious
    aspects—Christianity. | Control (Psychology—Religious
    aspects—Christianity.
Classification: LCC BV4598.2 .A78 2016 | DDC 248.4—dc23 LC record available at
https://lccn.loc.gov/2016023300

Printed in the United States of America

23   22   21   20   19   18
 8   7   6   5   4

CONTENTS

Introduction

WE COMMEND YOU for picking up this book. Your interest shows an awareness that your life can be better and that something needs to change in order for this to happen. Maybe you've tried other things that haven't worked, and maybe you don't have a lot of hope that things can actually get better. But that's where *we* come in.

Numerous formulas and plans are available to help you find healing, purpose, and meaning—and we've written a few of them ourselves. Such plans and formulas will succeed *if* you can work them. But it's not easy to follow a plan if something or someone has a hold on your life. If there is a force within you or around you that continues to exert power over your life—power that overwhelms your best intentions, sabotages your greatest efforts, and frustrates your deepest desires—then no formula or set of keys or steps will help you until you are able to *take your life back*. True freedom comes when you gain the strength to no longer live in reaction to the negative power whose destructive control has kept you from living the life you were meant to live.

When I (Steve) was a young man, a force within me controlled everything in my life. It derailed the use of every talent, gift, and skill I possessed. It saturated my life with a deep darkness and the most penetrating pain imaginable. At times, it kept me locked in my room and stuck in my bed. There were days when my only goal was to break the oppressive bondage long enough to get out of bed, stand up, and walk farther than the bathroom—at least to the kitchen, where I could catch a glimpse of outside light.

The hold on my life was so strong and so powerful that it almost killed me. I'll tell you more about that later in the book, but for now, suffice it to say that I have seen the pit from the inside.

The force that controls your life may be similar to the one that controlled mine. And it may be destroying any potential for joy or meaning to rise up in your life. If you're at all like I was, you may feel all bound up with *shame*—and until you take command of it and remove it from the center of your world, nothing will ever get better. But don't despair. That's why we're here to help you.

Because shame is so common and so destructive, we want to establish right here in the introduction that our desire—our goal— is for you to read this book without experiencing even a single pang of shame for where you are, where you've been, or what you've been through. Both of us (Steve and David) have had to deal with our own deep-seated shame. And just like you, most likely, we both have experienced some form of shaming from well-meaning professionals whose perspective and approach seemed so far above and beyond where we'd been. If you desire something better and want to take a significant step toward living differently, you can be assured that we're walking the pathway to freedom right along with you. We will show you how to move from reactive attitudes and behaviors to a place where you can *choose your response* to what life brings your way.

Not all shame is bad. Sometimes it motivates people to make good and necessary changes. But shame that comes from abuse, rejection, abandonment, neglect, or judgment—or even from well-meaning professionals—can infuse horror and self-loathing into the soul. That's the kind of shame we will help you get rid of—with some cooperation on your part—and replace with hope and healing, along with renewed purpose, vision, and meaning. We want to help you take charge of your past and your current circumstances so that you can look forward with confidence and faith to the road ahead.

Even if you're skeptical, believing that nothing can help and that this book will probably be no different from any other, at least you're still reading—you're still searching, still hoping. If you're not quite willing to buy in just yet, or if you're not sure you're willing to do what it takes to change, don't worry. Willingness is an acquired taste. It takes time, and it may not come easily. But if you're simply willing to stay with us, we will help you get the rest of the way by first eliminating the hold that destructive forces or influences have on your life. We will help you see your struggle from a different perspective, and we'll help you change the things that you have the power to change. As we help you take your life back, we hope and pray that any shame you still bear will melt away.

Thank you for allowing us an opportunity to help you. We have written several books together, but never with a greater desire to see people like you find hope, healing, meaning, purpose, and transformation. May God greatly bless you, and may you experience his presence as you read the following pages and begin to experience the life you were born to live.

PART I

The Reactive Life

1

THE PRODIGAL ON THE OTHER SIDE OF THE PALACE

WE'VE HEARD THE story of the prodigal son many times: the young man who insults and disgraces his father by demanding an early inheritance; who moves away from his father, lives it up, burns it up, comes crashing down, and eventually has to move in with some pigs—the ultimate symbol of unclean and destitute living. The term *prodigal* has come to characterize anyone who has ever acted out— through addiction, rebellion, recklessness, promiscuity, or any number of other destructive behaviors—and people who have surrendered ownership of their lives to an external controlling influence. For these prodigals—a group that includes both men and women, sons and daughters—the Bible says "their god is their appetite" and their focus is woefully shortsighted.[1] That's why the appetites that carry them away are often the very same appetites that bring them home again.

In the parable, the wayward son wakes up cold and hungry one morning and realizes that the servants back home have it better than he does—at least they have a roof over their heads and food on the table. So it isn't repentance, or even regret, that draws him home as much as it is simple hunger and poverty.[2] Still, he heads back, burdened with shame and rehearsing his appeal: "Father, I have sinned against both heaven and you, and I am no longer worthy of being called your son. Please take me on as a hired servant."[3] But when he arrives at his father's house—actually, before he even gets there—a remarkable thing happens. The father—whom the son has dishonored, insulted, and abandoned—comes running toward him, embraces and kisses him, and welcomes him home. There's no shaming, blaming, or even explaining to be done. The father simply enfolds him in his loving arms and calls for a celebration: "For this son of mine was dead and has now returned to life. He was lost, but now he is found."[4]

At the very center of taking your life back is a return to the Father who has been watching and waiting and hoping for you to come home.

At the very center of taking your life back is a return to the Father who has been watching and waiting and hoping for you to come home. There is no shame or recrimination, only celebration.

Maybe, after all you've done, it's hard for you to believe that anyone—much less God—would come running to you if you turned back toward home. That's precisely how scandalous this parable was in the ears of the people who heard it firsthand from Jesus. A wealthy landowner in those days would never have run anywhere. That would have been far beneath his dignity. Not only that, but the son had already dishonored his father by squandering his inheritance and running away. And yet the point of the parable is that God is always moving toward us, always calling us home, always ready to enfold us in his loving arms.

We expect judgment. God offers grace.

We expect condemnation. God responds with mercy.

We expect rejection. Jesus says, "Come to me, all of you who are weary and carry heavy burdens, and I will give you rest. Take my yoke upon you. Let me teach you, because I am humble and gentle at heart, and you will find rest for your souls. For my yoke is easy to bear, and the burden I give you is light."[5]

If you've been acting out, we encourage you to address those issues in your life. Even if it's your appetites—not love, repentance, or desire for connection—that bring you home, it simply proves that God can use the destructive things in our lives to bring us to the point of surrender. But only when you're willing to face up to your destructive behaviors will you even be able to begin taking your life back. If you will wake up and recognize where your decisions have taken you, and if you will return home to your heavenly Father, you will find him waiting to take you back in, just as the father in the parable is waiting and willing to welcome his son home.

That was my (David's) experience. Like many teens, I acted out all through high school. Once I was old enough to drive and got a car, I did whatever I wanted. My parents were powerless to stop me, so they just ignored everything. I knew that what I was doing was wrong, but I didn't care. I once felt guilty enough about what I was doing that I refused to take Communion, but I didn't change my behavior.

One day, while I was in high school, a friend and I downed a bottle of whiskey, and I spent the school day pretty well wasted. I was out of control, but nobody intervened. Finally, after I graduated, I confronted myself and decided that I was on the wrong path and that it was time to get things right with God. When I turned back to God, there was no shame or condemnation—only the open arms of God the Father welcoming me back.

Acting *In*
Maybe you can't identify with the prodigal son—you've done your best to live an upright life, and you've never acted out in self-destructive

ways. In fact, you don't have a lot of patience for people who have lost control of their lives and have gone down the wrong path. If that's the case, we encourage you to read the rest of the parable, where we're introduced to another brother, whose story may be easier to identify with.

In Rembrandt's well-known masterpiece *The Return of the Prodigal Son*, the brooding image of the elder brother dominates the right-hand side of the painting. The rich crimson fabric and embroidered edges of his robes establish his position as an insider, yet he stands emotionally distant and removed from the redemptive reunion of his father and brother. His hands are clasped under his robes, in stark contrast to the open, forgiving hands of his father.

The challenge for the elder brother is that he has done everything right, at least in his own eyes, and yet the abundant life that he believed was promised to him—and it *was*—has eluded him. All of his disappointment and frustration has turned inward, manifesting itself as anger, bitterness, hatred, judgment, jealousy, spite, envy, dissension, division, resentment, isolation, rejection, and abandonment. Having that much territory in the soul taken over by so many complicated, negative emotions doesn't leave much room for love or gratitude. Far from having ownership of his own life, he lives in bondage to disillusionment and to his own sense of entitlement. Any of us who have walked that emotionally destructive path have handed over our lives to the obsession of what feels wrong, unfair, disrespectful, or unresolved. The elder brother needs to take his life back every bit as much as the younger brother does. And it may be that the elder brother has the more difficult journey back to wholeness because so much of his pain has been stuffed down beneath the surface of his life.

The elder brother has done everything right, at least in his own eyes, and yet the abundant life has eluded him.

It's interesting that this story has been popularized as the parable of the prodigal son because Jesus didn't identify it that way. That title was added by someone along the way who was creating subheadings in the Bible text. If we were to name this story, it might just as easily be called the parable of the father's love or the parable of the angry brother.

We might also say that the elder brother is a prodigal in his own way. We've so often heard the term used to describe a rebellious child who has left the fold that it's easy to overlook the fact that the inward attitudes of the heart are what lead to the outward behaviors. The essence of being a "prodigal" is *wastefulness*. That includes wasting opportunities for good deeds and leaving valuable resources unused on the shelf.

The elder brother had so much at his disposal—"Everything I have is yours," his father said—and yet, in his resentment toward his younger brother's wild living, he hadn't availed himself of so much as a barbecued goat to celebrate with his friends. What a sad and shriveled life he chose for himself. But that isn't an uncommon way to live, especially when, as Christians, we're so busy keeping all the rules that we overlook the fact that God has given us the keys to his Kingdom. We're afraid that if we celebrate the return of wayward sons and daughters, we somehow condone their bad behavior: that forgiveness somehow equates with license. In the words of André Gide, we wonder, "Why more honor to a repentant sinner than to him . . . who has never sinned?"[6] In our self-righteous anger, we become people who look down on other people—or people who look down on people who look down on other people. As author and singer Sheila Walsh said recently, "Self-righteousness is a paper-thin disguise. All it takes is for one messed-up 'loser' to come wandering home and our claws come out."[7]

The wayward prodigal reacted to his pain and woundedness by looking for life outside the walls of his father's house. And though the elder brother stayed home, even he thought the key to a happy life was somewhere else.

Here's a vital truth: The life we desire is not "out there" somewhere. We have full access to everything belonging to God—right here, right now, right where we are. To live that abundant life, we must simply open our arms and unclench our grip on everything we've been so desperately trying to hold on to, and we must *recognize*, *receive*, and *accept* all that our heavenly Father has for us. That's the life for which we were saved. That's the life we need to take back.

To live that abundant life, we must simply open our arms and unclench our grip on everything we've been so desperately trying to hold on to.

What becomes apparent as we read this story is that neither son really knew his father. If either one had, he would not have felt the need to *act in* or *act out* in negative and destructive ways. Both sons would have been able to accept the father's generosity and would have been thankful for all that was available to them. But clearly, some kind of wounding had driven a wedge between the members of this family.

Most teachings you'll hear on the story of the prodigal son portray the father as a picture of God, and thus we assume there can be no failure on his part in these broken relationships because he is perfect. But if we keep our focus on the human scale, as Jesus does in his telling of the story, we gain a different perspective. As we'll see in the next chapter, every generation has been wounded in some way by the generations that came before it, and every generation passes that wounding on to succeeding generations. So from that standpoint, the father in this story also represents countless generations of the wounded, stretching all the way back to the original breach with our Creator and ultimate Father. Woundedness is a consequence of the Fall, and we all wear it in some fashion.

Reactive Living

If we picked up the latest issue of *Reactive Living* (if such a magazine existed), we might find a picture of the prodigal son's elder brother on the front cover. The caption might read, "What about me?" That's what the reactive life is all about. No matter what happens, we *react* in our own self-interest. If we feel threatened, diminished, or overlooked, we react. We want what's fair for us, and we don't really care about anyone else. We're in pain, and when anything touches our woundedness, we react. We're on high alert for both insult and injury, and whenever the internal siren goes off, we react. Just like the elder brother, we react when we don't get what we want, when we don't get what someone else gets, or when we're not recognized for how awesome and amazing we are. It's an ingrained reflex. Whether we've experienced a perceived slight or a direct insult, we're not able to *respond* because we don't have enough internal self-control to keep ourselves from *reacting*.

The elder brother had done everything right, as far as he could tell. He had been obedient; he hadn't run away; he hadn't embarrassed or humiliated his father. He had done what a dutiful child does, and he expected to be recognized and rewarded accordingly. In our most selfish moments, we are all just like him—jealous of anyone who gets a bigger dose of grace and feeling entitled to a celebration just for being alive. We've all been there, focused on what's happening on the other side of the palace rather than enjoying and being thankful for all the blessings we've been given.

The elder brother had done what a dutiful child does, and he expected to be recognized and rewarded accordingly.

When we're constantly looking at what's happening with other people and measuring our satisfaction based on how fairly we feel we've been treated, we are forever at the mercy of whatever is going on *over there*. We've wired ourselves to react to whatever scale of comparison we've established. If our dependency invites criticism, we react defensively to justify, minimize, and project our problems onto someone or something else. We may react with anger to drive someone away, or we may withdraw with a whimper to elicit sympathy.

These reactions are not always extreme, and they may not even be noticeable to other people. Our reactions are nuanced and variable, and we're able to adapt to the painful reality of our inner world and deflect attention away from ourselves and the source of our pain. After years of reactive living, we've carved a deep rut in which to run, and we're more afraid of what lies outside the rut than we are of staying stuck. When pressured or threatened, we react. And we stay stuck.

To be fair, our reactiveness is often rooted in pain that accrued when we were very young. Whether we were neglected, misunderstood, abandoned, used, abused, or tortured—or whether we experienced something equally horrific—we were truly victims. We learned to react negatively to others and to loathe ourselves. All of these attacks were undeserved, and at such an early age all we could do was survive. We weren't able to change anything. Even today, as adults, we have something within ourselves that resists the notion that meaningful change—much less complete transformation—is possible. We step back into the shadows because we don't have any proof that transformation can actually happen. So we continue to react to protect ourselves and whatever it is we think we have to lose.

The entire purpose for *Take Your Life Back* is to show you that real and lasting change *is* possible. Not only possible, but also achievable. At some point, we all must stop *reacting* and learn how to *respond* appropriately instead. If your life has been hijacked, it's up to you to take it back, with God's help—and the sooner the better.

Stepping Out of the Shadows

In Rembrandt's famous painting, the elder brother hovers on the edge of decision. Will he recede into the shadows of his inward obsession, remaining captive to his anger and resentment; or will he step forward into the light and find healing even as he joins in his father's embrace of the one who has come home?

At any time, the elder brother could step out of the shadows and join the celebration. But he is stuck in his point of view, unable to see the situation from a different perspective. That's often what keeps people in bondage to *acting in.* If only he could reframe the picture and *see* it all through the eyes of his father, or *feel* it all through the heart of his prodigal brother, he might reawaken and take his life back free and clear.

For us, if we would see things from God's perspective (who sees the end from the beginning) or feel things with the heart of Jesus (who sacrificed everything to set us free), we could move from the dire picture painted in Philippians 3:19—headed for destruction, owned by our appetites, invested in our shame, and thinking only about life here on earth—to the promise of Philippians 3:20, which reminds us of our citizenship in heaven and our eager anticipation of Christ's return.

At any time, the elder brother could step out of the shadows and join the celebration. But he is unable to see the situation from a different perspective.

The elder brother's first step is to become aware of how he is feeling and how it affects his behavior. Change may begin with the realization that nothing he has been feeling is going to change anything. In fact, the more negative and angry he becomes, the less able he is to have a positive impact. Stewing in the residue of his bitterness changes nothing for the good. By accepting his own powerlessness, he might come to accept the frailties of his father and his brother as well.

He could try to understand what God is up to here. He could reframe the story from God's point of view and discover that he is merely a part of the story and not the whole story. He might feel some gratitude that he's alive and full of potential. And he might even find a way to feel some gratitude that his brother has survived and is safe at home. He could count his blessings and express his thankfulness to God. But for now we must leave him as Rembrandt has him: a proud and prominent figure standing paralyzed on the perimeter by the bitterness that clutches his heart.

The position of the elder brother in the painting suggests that Rembrandt was aware that there were two prodigals. One had lived outside the palace walls, and the other within. One had acted out; the other acted in. Both had abandoned love, and both needed the grace and mercy of the father. Both needed healing and restoration. It seems that Rembrandt was aware that the elder brother's restoration would be a much more difficult task than the younger brother's. It's much harder to change when we're looking down than when we are down and looking up.

An Open Invitation

God invites us every day to come out of the shadows and into the light. He wants us to have the courage to reach out to others despite our fears and insecurities. As we humble ourselves before God, he empowers us to reach outside of ourselves.

If you have been battered and bruised into submission, don't think that continuing to suffer will make you well or that more time will produce a different result. What we need isn't *in* us. It comes *from* God *to* us *through* others.

God invites us every day to come out of the shadows and into the light. He invites us to take back our lives.

Stepping out of the shadows is the first responsible move we can make toward recovery and redemption. That means acknowledging the problem and accepting our powerlessness. God promises to guide us and empower us, but our part of the equation is *responsible action*. Even in the worst of situations, we're called to make the best of things, to do what we can to move toward wholeness. There is no life so painful that it absolves us of our obligation to pursue responsible living. Sooner or later, those painfully responsible actions become routine, and they bring with them security and hope, healing and redemption.

Maybe you have felt that you are without options. Maybe you've been so controlled by circumstances or by another person that having the freedom to choose for yourself seems impossible. Maybe you've resigned yourself to living life at the mercy or behest of another. If so, when you make the choice to get out or get better, it may feel weird or strange or even wrong. Even though it will be better, it may not feel like it at first. But the consequences of choosing to change are a better life and a better outlook. You must work through the discomfort of getting better so that you can find the abundant life you were meant to live.

On the other hand, if you choose not to get better, that choice has consequences as well—destructive consequences. We often think it's better to wait than to move ahead. Too much risk. Too much work. Too much pain. We think that if we can hold on wherever we are, something will finally break us out and set us free. But it doesn't work that way; such thinking only wastes valuable time.

Perhaps you see yourself as a prodigal who needs to come home. Come on home. Maybe you now recognize yourself as the elder sibling who has the more difficult journey toward health and wholeness. But no matter where you are or what you've been through, God wants to help you take your life back so you can live freely with him and for him. You have not gone too far or resented too intensely. God's invitation to take your life back is always there, awaiting your response. Let's begin the healing journey.

2

UNDERSTANDING
YOUR WOUNDEDNESS

WE DEVELOP "ELDER SIBLING SYNDROME" unconsciously and involuntarily. It's not something we choose. We lose ourselves to avoid dealing with our own pain. But how did we get on this painful path in the first place? For most of us, the trail was blazed by the degree to which we were wounded as children. We talk about "degrees of woundedness" because we all were wounded to some extent as children, some of us more deeply than others. But to whatever degree we were wounded, our response was to hide our real self and develop a false, reactive self as a cover. In order to avoid being aware of and feeling the pain of our woundedness, we now hide the parts that feel the most authentic or vulnerable. And not only do we hide these parts from other people, but we also hide them from ourselves. They get buried. Before long, the only things visible are the facades we've created—some of them more artful than others.

The Battle between Our False Self and Our Real Self

To understand the difference between what we refer to as the *real self* and the false selves we often construct for different situations or relationships, we must begin by looking at Adam and Eve in the Garden of Eden. Like us, they were created in the image of God. "God created human beings in his own image. In the image of God he created them; male and female he created them."[1] Each person is a unique creation, made in God's image for the purpose of having a relationship with God and with other people.

At the very beginning, both Adam and Eve were living only in their real selves. At Creation, there was a sense of oneness between them that we see most clearly when God introduces Eve to Adam. When Adam responds, "This one is bone from my bone, and flesh from my flesh,"[2] he is noticing only how much Eve is like him—he's not fixated on their differences. He felt a sense of completeness of himself in Eve.

At the very beginning, Adam and Eve were operating only in their real self. At creation, there was a sense of oneness between them.

"Now the man and his wife were both naked, but they felt no shame."[3]

In the beginning, Adam and Eve were operating through their true and authentic selves—as God's perfect creation. There was no hiding, only spontaneous love for each other. They were free with their feelings and were not defensive about anything—all of which are characteristics of the real self, as God intended. In addition, as God planned, his created beings were made to be caring; to be able to play and have fun, with a childlike openness to life; and to be vulnerable with each other. And they were made to form a real and deep connection with each other. In all, they were intended to live authentically as real selves with others and with their Creator. This was the reality of who they were meant to be.

To review, here are some of the positive attributes of our real self:

POSITIVE ATTRIBUTES of OUR REAL·SELF

» Living authentically, with no pretense

» Able to be spontaneous

» Caring for and loving others

» In touch with one's own feelings

» Free to play and have fun

» Able to accept nurturing from others

» Open and not defensive

» Able to be vulnerable

» Accepting of oneself

Then Eve chose to abandon her real self and her real-self connection with Adam. She began to have private conversations with a serpent, in a way that was separate and distinct from who she really was. She fell into the temptation of creating an all-knowing, all-powerful, and independent false self, apart from Adam. Her response did not reflect her true self as being one with Adam. Instead, she immediately created a disconnected, false self, focused on building an identity of knowledge and power outside of her companion's knowledge. But the real self was always there.

The real self, quite simply, is the self that God sees. He sees it all, with all its flaws. He does not approve of or endorse everything he sees, but he loves the person he sees. He does not see an idealized self, free of sin. He sees the real self—sinful, doubtful, and flawed—and yet he accepts the reality of it and loves us in spite of it all.

The real self is the self that God sees—sinful, doubtful, and flawed—and yet he accepts the reality of it and loves us in spite of it all.

In coming to rediscover and understand your real self, you must ask the following questions: What does God see? What is there that is good? What is there that is flawed? What defective means of living have I chosen that have attempted to conceal me from others and from God? How do I surrender those defective ways and start working on repairing, reviving, and restoring my real self so that I can feel a deep and rich connection with God and with everyone who enters into a relationship with me?

Before Adam and Eve disobeyed, Eve abandoned her real self and discovered that the promise of a quick path to becoming something more than ourselves never works, especially when we leave behind the God who created us and the relationships God created for us. Adam, for his part, seemed to abandon his real self without a thought.

When Adam and Eve disobeyed God, everything changed. They began living their lives out of touch with their real selves. Instead, they set in motion a pattern that has been replicated by everyone ever since, as we spend our lives developing false selves to hide behind. At the very moment when Adam and Eve disobeyed, "they suddenly felt shame at their nakedness. So they sewed fig leaves together to cover themselves."[4] Then, when God asked them why they had hidden from him, Adam replied, "I was afraid because I was naked."[5]

Suddenly, the innocence they had enjoyed was lost, and they began to blame each other for their problems. Instead of being governed by the real, authentic selves that had been created in the image of God, they now operated out of selves that were rooted in shame and fear. They no longer enjoyed the open, joyful, and unencumbered relationship they had shared with God and with each other.

The effect of shame and fear

As we look at the various forms of wounding we can experience, we'll see that a very common response is to be ashamed and fearful. We blame our fear and shame on others, and we also begin to blame ourselves—our real self, which we now believe is defective and must be hidden. In its place, we put forward a false, reactive self that is defensive, fearful, and closed down. No longer oriented toward God's truth and our real self, we worry about what other people will think of us (if they think of us at all), and we don't trust anyone to look out for our best interests. In our relationships, we become manipulative, self-protective, and defensive.

We also begin to put distance between ourselves and others for fear they will see past our false self and expose the defective nature of our true self. That can lead us to be very controlling and self-righteous. We don't play much anymore for fear of lowering our guard and being uncovered. And we keep a careful watch on our feelings, so we're never caught off guard.

Our unique false self

By the time we are adults, we have carefully designed our false self to replace our buried real self. Each false self has a core issue that we depend on to protect ourselves from being known. For some it is control; for others, it is trust issues. Some design a false self that is adept at avoiding feelings. Some who struggle with abandonment issues create a false self to guard against further abandonment, while others seek to become totally self-sufficient so that they won't need anything from anyone. It is not a happy way to live.

In order to take back your life, you must unbury your real self. This means you must face the pain of your woundedness, grieve what has been lost, make peace with what was taken from you, and embrace the real *you* that God created. When God looks at you, he sees past the false selves and longs to relate again to your real self. He didn't make a mistake when he made you. May we once again rejoice as the psalmist rejoices: "Thank you for making me so wonderfully complex! Your workmanship is marvelous—how well I know it."[6]

The Setting for Our Wounding

Our wounding begins as soon as we are born into this imperfect world. Think of the extreme contrast between the quiet safety of the womb, where every need is met automatically, and the terror that every newborn must experience at some level as he or she is suddenly brought into a strange and very unsafe world. Now our needs will be met in a somewhat random manner. We can't talk; we can only cry when we have a need. And parents have varying abilities to interpret those cries.

Our need for safety and security is met during the early months of life by our connection to the mothering person who cares for us. Our single task during this time is to snuggle into the world represented by that nurturer, who is there to make us feel safe.

But at around six months of age, another basic need springs up in opposition to our need for safety. We begin to notice our arms, feet, toes, fingers, and especially thumbs. Gradually, we begin to realize that "I am a *me*," separate from the mothering person. And thus begins a three- or four-year journey of trying—at first, without words—to differentiate between ourselves as separate individuals and the *we* of "Mommy and me." These two competing tasks—connection and attachment versus separation and independence—create a fertile environment for our being wounded at a time in our lives when we don't have adequate words to express our feelings, needs, frustrations, and fears.

Our wounding begins as soon as we are born into this imperfect world.

What's interesting about the struggle between attachment and independence in early childhood is that it leaves unfinished business for later resolution. The competing needs generally reach equilibrium during our elementary school years, only to reemerge with a vengeance—but not always with greater articulation—during our teens. As adolescents, the struggle is broadened to how we can continue to be part of our family while at the same time moving more in the direction of independence. In midlife, we wrestle with these competing issues again in a different context and then one more time as we reach old age.

Because we were not able to express ourselves verbally for much of the early childhood period, the burden fell to our parents to assist us by determining which of the two tasks we were struggling with at any given time. Did we need more love and connection or more room to explore the world independently? Such naturally conflicting needs and objectives created all kinds of opportunities for misunderstanding and misapplication and opened our tender souls to inevitable wounds, whether well-intentioned or otherwise.

Our Parents' Part in Wounding

The starting point for understanding our woundedness is to recognize that our parents—and their parents before them—were also wounded people to some degree. We all are sinful human beings raised by other sinful human beings, and we all fall short in some way. Some families create and pass down a healthier home environment, and thus the wounding may not be as obvious; but everyone is still wounded in some way. Perfect parents don't exist. For those of us who came from chaotic, dysfunctional families, our wounds are just more obvious.

As children, we didn't think of our parents as being wounded. We simply experienced as normal whatever they did and said. As adults, we often excuse our parents' shortcomings by saying, "They did the best they could." But "the best they could" was never enough to keep them from wounding us. Our parents all fell short, and those of us who are parents have also fallen short, if for no other reason than that we were wounded by our wounded parents and have operated out of that woundedness.

Some parents do better than others, but no parent does a perfect job. In fact, those who try too hard to be perfect may raise entitled, self-righteous kids who are difficult to live with as adults. The good parents are the ones who are "just good enough." Though the parents' mistakes may add to their

No parent does a perfect job. The good parents are the ones who are "just good enough."

feelings of inadequacy—which is part of what they pass along to their children—those same mistakes may help the children grow strong and healthy, depending on how the children respond. If parents focus too much on their mistakes, it may make them even more apt to wound their children. Or it may prompt the children to defend their parents as a way of minimizing their own woundedness.

When parents struggle to hide their woundedness, they can end up projecting their brokenness onto their children. They may criticize their children for something they see in themselves, but they can't or won't acknowledge that they themselves are struggling. Where they feel inadequate, they see the same inadequacies reflected in their children.

One common form of wounding that families readily pass from one generation to the next is the sense of never truly feeling accepted by the father. Whether the father abandoned the family emotionally or was simply very critical of them, the children grew up believing that his love, acceptance, and approval were unattainable. No wonder so many people have a messed-up view of God, our ultimate Father.

Children who experience constant criticism while growing up are more likely to pass that critical spirit along to future generations. The woundedness of one generation becomes the woundedness of the next, and each successive generation buries the pain along with the wound. And because the pain is buried and embedded in our emotions, the wounding of generations happens inadvertently. An example would be the man who felt incapable of ever measuring up to his father's expectations. Whether he was trying to help his father paint the house or working to improve his grades at school, his efforts were never quite good enough. The painful part was realizing that his father wasn't even aware of the effect of his critical words. The son simply accepted it as being his father's way.

When the son became a father himself, he vowed that he would be different with his own children. But while fixing a leaky faucet in the bathroom, with his young son trying to assist him, he heard himself say, "You're no help; I'll take care of it." Later, he realized that he had passed his own father-wound on to his son, but like his father before him, he never apologized or said anything about it to the boy.

Both of my (David's) parents were deeply wounded people. My father was born in Ireland and lost his own father when he was thirteen. My dad was the youngest in his family, and as I learned years later, it was an Irish tradition that the youngest son would take care of his widowed mother until she either remarried or died.

My grandmother was a big, dominating farm woman who ran my dad's life for the next twenty years. She wouldn't let him date, marriage was out of the question, and she constantly checked up on where he was and what he was doing. My father never spoke of her, and I didn't even know her name until after he died.

When my dad was finally free of his mother, he was determined that no one would ever control him again. After marrying at the age of thirty-five, he shut down and became emotionally unavailable. But that was okay with my mom because she, too, was emotionally closed down after losing her mother at the age of three. Her father remarried when she was nine, and she became a real-life Cinderella— but no fairy godmother ever appeared to rescue her from her cruel stepmother.

That was my home environment: Two wounded parents had withdrawn into themselves for survival, and I was left to raise myself.

The Child's Part in Wounding

We can't place all the blame on the parents, for children also participate in the process of wounding. All children see their parents, even hurtful parents, in an idealized way. After all, Mom and Dad are the only parents they've ever known, and children need their parents. I (David) can remember thinking, when I was ten or eleven years old, that my real parents were going to come and rescue me from the imposters I was living with. I didn't want to be an orphan; I simply wanted relief from the way my parents treated me. In my fantasy, my real parents would come and take me to Switzerland, which seemed like an ideal setting. But like any child, I needed to have parents.

From an early age, we work hard at keeping our parents in the "good" category, regardless of how bad they may actually be. It's about survival. How can young children survive if they see their parents as inadequate or bad? They can't. Some theorists have suggested that this defense of the parent is operational even in the first months of a child's life. For example, when a baby cries from hunger and the mother comes and changes the baby's diaper, the child may internalize the blame for the mother's mistake: "I guess I didn't cry the 'I'm hungry' cry. It's my fault!"

From an early age, we work hard at keeping our parents in the "good" category, regardless of how bad they may actually be.

It's normal for young children to idealize their parents. Over time, this pattern becomes deeply ingrained, and as the children continue to try harder, they also blame themselves for any problems that arise.

As the children strive to help their parents be good parents, their emerging sense of their own real self begins to be buried. Because children think in dichotomies of all good or all bad, they assume ownership of all the bad as a way to keep their parents good. To preserve this delicate and often volatile balance, children try to act in ways that are "helpful." When Mom gets upset, the child tries to comfort her. When Dad yells at Mom, the child holds on to Mom as reassurance that "somebody cares."

Children also naturally believe what their parents tell them—

including what their parents say about them and about other people. I (David) remember working with a woman named Katherine, who kept saying that she was stupid even though she had advanced degrees from a prestigious university and worked in a very demanding profession. As I asked her questions, trying to understand how she could feel that way, Katherine suddenly began to remember examples of how her mother had told her she was stupid. She recalled a specific event when she had spilled a glass of milk and her mother had raged at her. These memories had been buried along with her real self.

As we continued to talk, many more examples popped into her consciousness of statements her mother had made to her and about her—a consistent pattern of calling her stupid. Though she was now a successful middle-aged woman who was anything but stupid, Katherine still believed and acted on what her mother had said years ago. Although the actual statements had been deeply buried in her subconscious, and although she had forgotten the source of her beliefs, she had never forgotten the message.

Over the years, Katherine's attempts to avoid the pain of her woundedness were channeled into academic pursuits and her career. It was her way of burying her real self. She created a false self that tried hard to pretend she wasn't stupid, but part of her still believed what her mother had said. She may have convinced others with her confident outward appearance, but she remained unconvinced herself until she brought her woundedness back into her consciousness, worked on recovering her real self, and began to take her life back.

Classic Dependency

What we have just described is commonly known as classic dependency, or codependency. The problem begins with the way we seek to avoid the pain that resulted from the wounding that we experienced as children and were unable to deal with because it involved our parents. This pain was an internal experience that embedded itself in our emotions. As ill-equipped children, our only strategy was to bury the pain, not realizing that we were also burying our real self, our very soul. From there we developed external coping strategies designed to keep us from ever touching the pain, and we set about trying to fix other people's problems.

The consequence of this deep emotional suppression is that we eventually lose touch with our inner life. Instead of experiencing a full range of emotionally healthy feelings as human *beings*, we become human *doers*. Everything in our lives becomes based on performance, to the point where we no longer know what we truly feel. Instead, we struggle with emotions of anger, fear, emptiness, shame, and numbness. Obviously, these feelings are painful as well, but we anesthetize them by focusing elsewhere, poking our noses into other people's problems while neglecting our own. Even those whose problems we are trying to fix, such as the alcoholic, struggle with the issue of dependency underneath their addictive behaviors.

Dependency itself is an addiction. In order to recover, the dependent must eventually come to terms with the same issues caused by any other type of addiction.

In truth, dependency itself is an addiction, and in order to recover, the dependent person must eventually come to terms with the same issues caused by any other type of addiction.

Though we as codependents are focused on taking care of other people, we are actually attempting to restore a sense of safety and security to our internal world. As adults, we may try to prevent conflicts and upheaval in our relationships by appeasing others. But as long as our focus is on the externals, we will never resolve the internal root issues.

Classic dependency can be summarized as follows:

» It is acquired early in life.
» It is a pattern of learned behavior.
» It is developmental.
» It focuses on externals.
» It is chronic—it won't "just go away."
» It is a progressive problem—that is, it gets worse.
» It causes us to worry about being seen as selfish or controlling.
» It causes us to worry about being liked by others.
» It seeks to keep the peace at any cost to ourselves.
» It requires us to monitor the moods of others.
» It causes us to be too trusting of others.
» It makes excuses for the other person.
» It easily sacrifices for others but not for ourselves.
» It is an addiction.

Secondary Dependency

If you were raised in a healthier home environment, you may not relate completely to the discussion of classic dependency. When you look inside yourself, it may be hard to come up with deeply painful experiences. Or maybe you were the type of child known as *resilient*, who isn't affected as deeply by painful childhood experiences. In either case, the dependent behaviors expressed in your life, though still present, may be less severe.

Adults from healthier backgrounds can still develop dependent patterns of behavior. For example, if you are in a significant relationship with someone who is actively addicted or extremely dysfunctional, it's easy to focus on those issues until you develop a full range of dependent behaviors. After all, an addiction demands attention from the other people in the addict's life. And if that attention is reactive, soon all the caretaking behaviors will be there. If you continue in that relationship, eventually there will be no difference between your actions and those of a classic codependent.

The difference between classic and secondary dependencies can be seen in how long it takes for recovery and in the focus of that recovery. Those with a secondary dependency seem to recover more quickly than those who are classically codependent. Instead of digging into their childhood to see how the real self was lost, people needing to recover from secondary codependent patterns will seek to understand their adult relationships. Either way, however, some form of life recovery work will be necessary.

Life Recovery

To begin the work of taking your life back, you must first get in touch with the buried pain if you are a classic dependent. If you are seeking to take your life back as a secondary dependent, you must get in touch with how and why you were drawn into your relationship with the needy person. Either way, it's not going to be easy, because most of us have spent years trying to either avoid or cover up the pain. We've also spent years practicing and incorporating into our lives the behavioral patterns of codependency.

To begin the work of taking your life back, you must first get in touch with the buried pain.

Part of the work necessary for taking your life back will require the help of others, even though no one else can fully understand the depth of your pain. And because pain is a relative experience, you may be afraid that others will try to minimize your pain. As you share your journey in the process of regaining your real self, remember that nothing hurts as much as your own pain. But in order to recover, someone else must be able to understand and feel your pain, and you must understand it as well. It always takes someone else to help us find our buried pain and also to validate the pain we've tried for so long to avoid.

Taking your life back also requires that you be open and honest with yourself and with someone else about what happened to you to create the dependent patterns of behavior.

Along the way, you will seek to identify the destructive behavioral patterns you have chosen to help you avoid your pain. You will break free when you're courageous enough to share your pain and make yourself accountable to someone. You can start by looking at the ways in which you've been wounded.

3

WHERE DOES
IT HURT?

WE'VE ALL BEEN WOUNDED in some way, and we've reacted to that wounding with various methods of acting out or acting in. But the common denominator is that we all have lost touch with our real self and have created false selves to help us survive and cope. We want to be more specific now and look at five primary ways in which many of us were wounded. All of these involve our being abused to some degree.

We realize that not everyone was explicitly abused during his or her growing-up years. But as you read through the descriptions of the five types of abuse, you may identify subtle elements of abuse that may have affected you and may have been part of your wounding. If you believe this chapter doesn't apply to your experience, that's not a problem. In subsequent chapters, we're going to look at other ways in which wounding can occur.

Mental Abuse

Mental abuse can be hard to identify because it's so subtle. Yet for many of us, it's how our woundedness began. Starting when we were very young, and long before we had developed the necessary interpretive and expressive skills to make sense of it all, we began to bump up against other people—primarily our closest family members and caretakers—who themselves were navigating life with various degrees of unresolved pain. Though differing in scope and intensity from family to family, some measure of woundedness was naturally passed along to us.

As children, our natural neediness made us susceptible to fears of abandonment by the most important people in our lives. Out of their own wounds, our parents invalidated our individuality and stifled our inner life of feelings. We gradually began to interpret our emotional life as being wrong or even toxic.

For example, Katherine, the woman we mentioned in the previous chapter who thought she was stupid, developed feelings of inadequacy and self-loathing as the result of mental abuse. Her mother likely had no idea that she was wounding her daughter, in part because she herself had been mentally abused as a child. And because the grandmother had died by this time, Katherine's mother wasn't able to talk with her own mother about her childhood. What Katherine remembered, however, was that her mother always tried to avoid being around her grandmother. It was not a loving relationship, and it was easy to see how the mental abuse of one generation had been passed along to the next.

What makes it all worse for children is that there's nothing they can do about it. After all, in most families, children have no say, and anything they say can be used against them and would only make things worse. Because children instinctively know, or soon find out, that they have no power to correct things, they end up feeling inadequate, ashamed, and bad. Children use the early defense mechanism of "splitting," in which they divide everything into categories of *all-good* or *all-bad*. And because they have to reserve the "all-good" category for their parents, on whom they depend for their survival, it leaves the "all-bad" category for themselves. Many still struggle with that dichotomy as adults, thinking that their parents are still always right and that they are still the bad ones.

We work on our external lives in order to avoid having to confront the wounded inner life that is filled with too much pain.

In order to cope emotionally with being "the bad guy," we must silence our real self. And then we try to fill the void by focusing on taking care of others. We work on our external lives in order to avoid having to confront the wounded inner life that is filled with too much pain.

Everyone experiences—and internalizes—some degree of mental abuse simply by being born into the human race. That fact alone explains why so many people seek fulfillment by taking care of other people. But for many of us, the cycles of abuse expanded.

Emotional Abuse

As with mental abuse, emotional abuse is often called the invisible wound because there are no physical scars or bruises to substantiate it. For that reason alone, it can cause devastating harm to the soul, destroying a child's sense of self and natural self-confidence. Think of the confusion a child feels when being emotionally abused. The natural response is to trust what the parents do and believe what the parents say, even though it is incongruent with the child's experience.

At first, the child feels an inner tension—*Do I trust and believe my parents or listen to my real self?*—but eventually the parents win the battle, and the child begins to dismiss his or her own questions and doubts.

Typically, emotional abuse accompanies physical or sexual abuse, but each of the three destroys the child's developing sense of self. The longer the abuse continues, the emptier the child's sense of self will become.

Emotional abuse can be subtle—as in sarcasm, verbal put-downs, or ridicule—or it can be openly violent, as in yelling, humiliation, and open cruelty. It is often explained away as being done out of love, but there is nothing loving about emotional abuse or any other kind of abuse.

Emotional abuse can also take the form of neglect, or lack of interest by the parent. Whether this indifference is expressed openly and aggressively toward the child—"Get out of here and leave me alone" or "I don't have time for you"—or passively through absence or lack of attention, it pervasively and systematically undermines and attacks the child's sense of identity and self-worth.

Children don't come into the world with a ready-made sense of self. Identity is formed through meaningful attachments and relationships. At first, an infant is simply an extension of the mothering parent. By the time they are two, children have begun to explore what it means to be a separate self. This developmental stage is sometimes called "the terrible twos," but it could just as easily be called "the wonder-full twos," as the child's unique personality emerges through curiosity and exploration.

Once the groundwork of identity has been established in early childhood, our felt need to find out who we are subsides until the teenage years. Then the search begins anew—often with a vengeance. *Who am I? How do I make sense of how I think and feel compared to what I see and hear?* Both the terrible twos and the teenage years are sensitive times developmentally, and emotional abuse can be especially damaging during these years.

Both of these stages are important in our search for a healthy sense of self. Abuse during these pivotal years can stunt our emotional development and hinder our ability to express ourselves in healthy ways. Sadly, we may become the negative persons that our abusers have accused us of being.

Here are some ways in which emotional abuse sometimes occurs:

» We were consistently made to feel worthless.
» Our point of view was consistently ignored.
» We were subjected to guilt or shame to make us comply.
» Our feelings were ignored.
» We were often given the silent treatment.
» We lived with a raging parent, whose rage was often directed at us.
» We were also physically or sexually abused.
» We often experienced sarcasm and ridicule.
» We were often criticized for what we did or didn't do.

This list is not exhaustive, but it highlights common examples of emotional abuse.

Physical Abuse

If you've ever seen pictures of a battered woman or an abused child, you may have wondered how anyone could be so cruel to another human being, let alone to a child. But we know it happens all too frequently. In *The Great Santini*, author Pat Conroy uses a fictional story to describe how abusive his father—the real-life Great Santini— had been to his family. But his father went to his grave insisting he had never been abusive.

In a more recent nonfiction book, *The Death of Santini*, Conroy spells out the extent of the abuse and how he first told his wife "the whole story of my father's long, debilitating war against his family."[1]

I had never revealed to another soul that he had been beating my mother since I was conscious of being alive, and that I remember hating him when I was in a high chair, my face burning with shame and humiliation that I could do nothing to protect my mother. My father could sense my hatred of him, and he began to beat me with some regularity when I was still in diapers.[2]

Conroy describes a scene from his childhood when his father choked him and banged his head against the wall. When, as an adult, he reminded his father of that incident, his father laughed and denied it ever happened, even though Pat told him that he could show him the damaged wall.

It's hard to believe his father's denial system was so strong that he could laugh it all off and deny everything, and children raised in a home like that might begin to question their own sanity. Indeed, Pat Conroy refers to his sister Carol Ann's psychotic break and how she "spent her days tormented by voices and visions and hallucinations."[3] Or they may have come to see the physical abuse as somehow normal. That was my (David's) experience as I grew up. My father had a violent Irish temper, and trips to the basement with him were often very unpredictable. But his explanation for the abuse was that it was "standard discipline."

If you wonder whether something that you experienced was abusive, ask yourself whether you would do the same thing to one of your own children.

I had an ulcer at the age of ten, which the doctor blamed on my diet. I believed that until I was in my forties. But if you had come to talk to me at the clinic about an ulcer, I never would have blamed it on your diet. I would have begun to explore the stress levels in your life. Still, for years I was unable to apply the same professional judgment and analysis to my own situation. It honestly never occurred to me that the stress of living with my dad's temper could have had anything to do with my ulcer. That's how normalization and rationalization work.

Not only do the parents deny the abuse, but even the abused child is subject to denial.

If you wonder whether something that you experienced was abusive, ask yourself whether you would do the same thing to one of your own children or condone other people doing the same thing to their children. Today, in an effort to avoid even a hint of physical abuse, many parents will not even spank their children.

Sexual Abuse

It wasn't very many years ago that sexual abuse was largely overlooked in our culture. Fortunately, that has changed, but it is still a crippling secret in far too many families. When it happens, it destroys the child's self-confidence, sense of worth as a person, and any sense of the safety of personal boundaries. When these children become adults, they often have no sexual boundaries, or they build walls that keep them from having healthy relationships.

Some people have a vague, distant sense that something bad happened but have no clear memory of an actual event. Others can remember the uncomfortable feeling of one of their parents (usually of the opposite sex) beginning to treat them as a surrogate spouse. Even when no sexual activity occurred, the child still experienced it as incestuous. This pattern of emotional entanglement can sometimes continue into the child's adulthood, and it represents an ongoing wound.

Studies have shown that memories of sexual abuse can be falsely implanted without the person even being aware. Old memories can also be influenced by subsequent events that may not be directly related, and not everything we recall may have happened exactly the way we remember it. So we must be careful with what we remember, especially in the area of sexual abuse, but that in no way diminishes the need to find constructive ways to work through these memories and the pain associated with them.

Both physical and sexual abuse destroy the natural boundaries of a child, and this can lead to boundary problems in adulthood. Wounded people tend to wound other people, and those whose personal boundaries were violated as children may tend to repeat the pattern, either openly or secretly. That's why, if you have been wounded by physical or sexual abuse (or both), it is essential that you take your life back.

Spiritual Abuse

Another form of abuse that isn't talked about very often is spiritual abuse. People who are recruited into cults are obviously spiritually abused. Jonestown in Guyana in 1978 and the Branch Davidian compound in Waco, Texas, in 1993 offer clear examples of spiritual abuse that also included emotional, physical, and sexual abuse. But what about something closer to home, such as churches where pastors misuse God's Word to control their congregations? These are a little more difficult to identify. But spiritual abuse exists, as counselor and theologian Jack Felton and I (Steve) describe in our book *Toxic Faith*.

Spiritual abuse is a counterfeit of true faith, based on distortions of God's Word.

Spiritual abuse is "a destructive and dangerous involvement in a religion that allows the religion, not a relationship with God, to control a person's life. . . . It is a defective faith with an incomplete or tainted view of God. It is abusive and manipulative and can become addictive."[4]

Spiritual abuse is a counterfeit of true faith, based on distortions of God's Word. When we are in an abusive environment, we come to believe the distortions about God and ourselves, as well.

When Jesus "became flesh and made his dwelling among us," he "came from the Father, full of *grace* and *truth*."[5] Healthy spirituality will always maintain a healthy balance between grace and truth. Grace is quite simply an expression of God's unfailing love—the kind of love described by the apostle Paul:

Love is patient and kind. Love is not jealous or boastful or proud or rude. It does not demand its own way. It is not irritable, and it keeps no record of being wronged. It does not rejoice about injustice but rejoices whenever the truth wins out. Love never gives up, never loses faith, is always hopeful, and endures through every circumstance.[6]

We don't deserve that kind of love, but God loves us anyway. That's grace in action.

This unfailing love is balanced by genuine truth. But truth is never put forward at the expense of grace, nor is grace ever given at the expense of the truth. They are always in exquisite balance. When they get out of balance, that's when spiritual abuse can occur.

Mental, emotional, physical, sexual, and spiritual abuse often occur in combination with each other because they all take advantage of our vulnerability and our need for connection. And they are at the root of classical codependency. When we have been abused in any or all of these ways, we lose a sense of our real self, and that's when we go looking for substitutes. Taking your life back begins with understanding the source of your woundedness. As the old *Living Bible* says, "You can't heal a wound by saying it's not there!"[7] Healing begins when we identify and understand our wounds.

The Roots of Secondary Dependency

What if, in looking back, you can honestly say there was no serious abuse when you were growing up? You may have been wounded in various ways, through trauma or difficult relationships, but there were no pervasive patterns and no one really to blame. Maybe you were profoundly misunderstood during your most formative years; or lost an important loved one at a critical juncture; or were dragged along on a traumatic, long-distance move at a time of increased vulnerability, such as the early teenage years; or participated in some way in a shaming or guilt-inducing incident that struck to the core of your identity and rattled your self-image. Your wounds may come from a more recent issue that you are dealing with; and though these wounds may be less persistent or pervasive, you believe they damaged or undermined your sense of self, and you still feel as if you need to take your life back.

When the source of our wounds is trauma, there is often a feeling of vulnerability that threatens our sense of identity.

When the source of our wounds is trauma, there is often a feeling of vulnerability that threatens our sense of identity, leading us to act in ways that might seem to promote healing and wholeness but that actually increase our sense of emptiness or fear. For example, if someone I loved suddenly left me or was taken from me, I would try to cover up my fear of further abandonment. But that wouldn't keep me from experiencing further abandonment. We'll look more closely at the effects of trauma in chapter 8.

The Wounding Edge of Narcissism

Another common situation is being in a committed relationship with someone who displays a lot of narcissistic tendencies.

The concept of narcissism is based on the Greek myth of Narcissus and Echo. Echo was a mountain nymph who loved to talk. But when she offended one of the gods, her punishment was that she could no longer speak except to repeat what others said. She is like the dependent in that she has no voice of her own, focusing only on what others say.

Echo fell in love with a young hunter named Narcissus and longed to tell him how she felt about him, but all she could do was echo what he said. Narcissus had also run afoul of one of the gods, and his punishment was to fall in love with the image of himself that he saw reflected in a pool of water as he leaned over to take a drink.

Once he became captivated, he had no eyes for Echo and could focus only on himself. It wasn't so much that he fell in love with himself, as some versions of the story suggest (in fact, narcissists really don't like themselves), but that he fell in love with his *image*—what others would see.

Because Echo had lost her sense of self and was unable to express her own thoughts, she developed an unhealthy dependence on taking care of Narcissus, with the hope that he would somehow see how much she cared for him.

To properly understand narcissism, we should place it on a continuum, ranging from healthy to unhealthy. We all have some degree of narcissism in us, some more than others. A healthy self-regard—which we all need—can be characterized by a wholesome self-love and self-concern, in which our needs and wants are in balance with the needs and wants of others. We have healthy boundaries that allow us to care for ourselves while also caring for other people.

The unhealthy narcissist is someone who doesn't care how his or her behavior affects other people. In fact, these narcissists have little or no insight into how they come across. This may manifest as simple arrogance, grandiosity, or a sense of entitlement. As a result, they use other people for their own purposes and expect to be cared for by others. Those at the unhealthy extreme of the spectrum have what is called a narcissistic personality disorder.

To stay in a relationship with someone who has a lot of narcissistic tendencies, you will either develop a classic case of dependency or you will become a secondary dependent.

To stay in a relationship with someone who has a lot of narcissistic tendencies, you will either develop a case of classic dependency or you will become a secondary dependent. This dependent behavior is required by the unspoken rules of relating to a narcissist—all of which are always attuned to the needs of the narcissist. To take your life back, you will need a lot of emotional and behavioral support from trusted people on your healing journey.

The Vortex of a Borderline Personality

Borderline personality disorder is another dysfunctional state that can cause us to become extremely preoccupied with the problems of another person. Nothing is ever comfortable in a relationship with this type of person. Sometimes he or she will be very needy and demanding, and then at other times he or she will push you away. We have to learn how to live with these extremes. With a person who has borderline personality disorder, the dependent is always having to repair some damage to the relationship caused by misreading the smoke signals. Sometimes the cues are contradictory: "Love me . . . don't love me . . . don't you dare not love me!" all at once.

People with borderline tendencies often have an exciting side to their personality. When they're *up*, they make "upness" contagious. They're fun to be with! But when they're down, it's easy to get sucked into the vortex of *down* or to wear ourselves out trying to help them get back up.

Borderline types are typically impulsive, and that can be part of the fun. But the more extreme they are, the more likely they are to blame others for everything bad that is happening in their lives. It is easy to see how the demands of living with someone like this would leave us with little time to care for our own needs. When we don't know what's coming next, we're always on edge, always on alert, always on call. In the end, we either lose ourselves in the relationship or we somehow get away.

Sorting the Puzzle Pieces

We don't bury our real selves on purpose or even by accident. We do it as a reaction to the pain of our woundedness or to the perpetual demands of someone close to us—whether it's a child, spouse, or parent. Taking your life back begins with identifying why you avoid your own self-care. Your woundedness and your dysfunctional relationships are pieces of that puzzle. Let's look now at a puzzle piece that determines how we react to the environment that led to our wounds and to the absence of our real self.

4

REACTING TO PAIN

WHENEVER I (STEVE) SPEAK at churches or other gatherings, I like to draw upon my life experience and find something either humorous or profound in it. In everything that happens in life, I figure there has to be a lesson, some laughter, and some evidence of the Lord's presence right in the middle of it.

I remember a trip to Babies "R" Us when my wife, Misty, was more than eight months pregnant with our first child. We were shopping for a chest of drawers for the nursery. When we found what we wanted, it was a little too heavy for me to handle on my own, so I asked for some assistance to load it into my truck. I never quite caught the name of the young man who came out from the back of the store to help me, but judging by his perfectly toned body and bulging muscles, it was probably something like Thor.

Thor was quite friendly and helpful, and everything went great—

until the very last second, when Thor, not realizing that my hand was still under the corner of the carton, dropped the chest onto the second finger of my right hand, which is only slightly less vulnerable and sensitive than the pinkie.

That momentary slip began a process of internal bleeding and swelling in my finger that would have to be relieved with a hot needle. My fingernail eventually fell off, and I wore cushioned protection on that hand for weeks afterward. But at the moment that it happened, even though the pain was quite intense, my immediate reaction was to hide the truth from Thor about the degree of my suffering.

Like his namesake in the Avengers, Thor had a kind and compassionate heart, and he immediately asked whether the instant compression of a two-hundred-pound walnut chest on my finger had hurt. What a nice young warrior-prince. I instantly responded as any fine young Christian man would. I denied the truth, lied to his face, and concealed my pain and discomfort. However, when my would-be helper wished me well and walked back into the store, I began a dance quite unlike any classical number you've ever seen. Staring in disbelief at my rapidly swelling and bruised finger, I wept uncontrollably, hopped around like a maniac, and uttered words not found in the Old or New Testament. It was not one of my better moments.

I denied my pain and tried to cover it up, even to the extent of lying about it, all so that I wouldn't appear weak.

About this time, Misty came out to the truck and asked what was wrong. I made the horrific mistake of saying something about my pain being worse than childbirth—which may still be an issue between the two of us ten years later. But it really did hurt.

Long after the pain had subsided, it occurred to me that my reaction that day was exactly the same as it had been my entire life. I denied my pain and tried to cover it up, even to the extent of lying about it, all so that I wouldn't appear weak. It was like second

nature to me. Though I was not abandoned as a child or emotionally abused, I felt very isolated and alone while I was growing up.
And I had never shared that feeling with anyone. My reaction to
the physical pain mirrored my reaction to all the emotional pain
I had endured during childhood. But now I know that I'm not alone.
Many, many people react to pain in the same way: denying it, hiding
it, and doing whatever they can to look as strong as possible.

Variations on a Theme

As we talk about reactions to pain in this chapter, we want to avoid
putting people into categories. No one likes to be reduced to a label.
Are we really so predictable and typical and easily identifiable that
everything about us can be summed up in a word or phrase? For a
lot of people, labeling can feel more demeaning than helpful. On the
other hand, it can be reassuring to know that other people have done
what we've done and have lived through it. Most important, though,
we want to help you see that how you've been reacting to pain has
allowed something or someone to take control of your life. If you can
see that, we know you can change it.

Our reactions to pain and our adaptations to it are unique to ourselves; we are not all the same. But we have several things in common:
In one way or another, we have turned our back on reality, and we
have allowed all, or portions, of our lives to be controlled by another
person, a destructive pattern, or unrealistic expectations. We live on
the edge of *almost*. We are almost breaking free, or we are almost free.
We are almost fed up or almost ready to take our lives back.

Here are some common signs that our lives are not our own. These
are all indications that we need to take action to take our lives back.

We deny

Some people would deny that they're in denial. They know there's a
problem. They see it perfectly. But denial is much more subtle and

complex than simply saying that what's there is not there, or than being unable to see what's there. We might *see* the problem, but we deny that we can do anything about it. Or we may compare ourselves to others and refuse to address our own problems until that really sick soul over there makes a move to get better. We refuse to admit that someone else's huge, enormous, too-big-to-be-missed problem does not eradicate our need to deal with our own issues. Denial is easy because we think we're in such better shape than that other person. By comparison, it appears that we're free. In truth, we are anything but free because we've allowed that person's glaring issues to blind us to our need to pursue our own recovery.

Denial keeps us from addressing the things we can change, causing us to think that our inability to change everything means we can't change anything.

Denial keeps us from addressing the things we can change, causing us to think that our inability to change *everything* means we can't change *anything*. Moreover, we deny that our reactions have become habitual, and we are unwilling to give them up, even though they keep everything the same or make things worse. Because we either don't or won't see how far we are from living the life that God intends for us, we stay in our denial and wait for the magic cure that never materializes.

But when we admit that we're in denial, and when we are willing to break through it, we can begin to move into recovery. Like the disabled man lying by the pool of Bethesda in John 5, we can pick up our mats and start to walk. We become curious about the things we don't see or understand. We begin to investigate the terrain of our lives. We might enlist a sponsor in a Life Recovery group to help us. A wise counselor who has helped others get their lives back on track may open the floodgates of hope for us. We might take an inventory of the defects we see in our lives and then review that inventory with someone else to validate what is real, what is exaggerated, and what we've been ignoring. Breaking out of our denial may be the first step toward seeing what is actually there in our lives—the aspects of our character and our circumstances that have been so distorted that we've become blind to them. None of this work will be easy, but as we move forward with purpose, we will feel an undeniable surge of hope rising in our hearts.

We minimize

Often, when we look at our problems, it's as if we're looking through the wrong end of a pair of binoculars. We view problems that are huge, that cannot be ignored or overlooked, as normal parts of our lives. We have become so accustomed to the bizarre realities of our lives that we see very little of what is actually there.

When we talk about the elephant in the room, we have a way of describing it as a small rodent. Our internal application for minimizing language automatically converts words like *pain* into *irritation*; *devastating* into *difficult*; *abusive* into *insensitive*; and *horrific* into *unpleasant*. Our self-talk is unrealistic, so whenever we communicate with someone else, we present our overwhelming problems as manageable situations that we have completely under control. Because we don't acknowledge the full scope and intensity of our struggles, we don't act in realistic ways to free ourselves and take our lives back. We minimize in order to give ourselves permission to do little or nothing to change.

Because we don't acknowledge the full scope and intensity of our struggles, we don't act in realistic ways to free ourselves and take our lives back.

We comply

After years of minimizing or outright denial, we have learned to fall in line and simply absorb whatever comes our way. If we are abused, we learn to take it. We comply as if it is our God-given duty to soldier on despite the pain. But it's not our duty; it's our *pattern*, our habitually destructive decision to go along with whatever is foisted on us or whatever we've fallen into.

We have made it our destiny to try to please the unpleasable. Our obsessions can't be analyzed enough, so we keep obsessing. Our compulsions are never satisfied; even though more than enough is never quite enough, we keep on doing and consuming the same things. We comply with the inner urge for more, more, more. We can become so lost that we find our identity in complying with the wishes and demands of others. We start to feel as if our entire purpose is to be used up, run over, stepped on, and put down. Our identity and our calling seem to merge into one demand: *Comply, go along, and don't make waves.*

We adhere

Some of us have spent so much time feeling abandoned and rejected that we will latch onto anyone who will have us, no matter how we're treated. We adhere to people who are very bad for us, as if we have no choice but to endure pain, suffering, or torture, because being attached to someone sick feels better than not being attached at all. Like diabetics eating nothing but sugar, we choose to consume the very things that will harm us. We hitch our lives to the very people who rob us of our lives. We become owned and operated by whatever we cling to in our desperate survival mode.

Stockholm syndrome is a term used to describe the phenomenon of hostages or victims of kidnapping who begin to bond with or identify with their captors. It was coined because of the actions of four hostages taken during a bank robbery in Sweden in 1973. The term came to prominence in the United States in 1974 when newspaper heiress Patty Hearst was kidnapped and soon afterward was seen in bank surveillance videos committing crimes alongside her captors. How could something so strange happen? We see examples of it all the time with abused children who not only stay with their tormentors but also come to defend them or at least rationalize their behavior. Another common example is a woman who clings to an emotionally and physically abusive husband or boyfriend, trying to meet his every need even as he robs her of everything good and wonderful about herself. Rather than run, she willingly cooperates as he cuts her off from her family and friends and cuts her down to a size he can manipulate and control. That is what it's like to adhere to a sick relationship rather than moving out and moving on to create a life free from control and manipulation.

We deceive

Even when the sadness of our lives is on full display, we don't see it because we are masters of deception. Like magicians, we make the visible invisible by refusing to face reality. We fill our souls with so many lies that eventually we lose the ability to see what is real and true about ourselves. Our self-deception manifests in a running stream of lies we tell ourselves and others: "There are no other options . . . God has abandoned us . . . we deserve this . . . this is the best we can do . . . he will change if I do more . . . she is just going through a phase . . . I am worthless . . . it's my duty to stay in this . . . no one can help me . . . no one understands me or my situation . . . this is normal . . . it will get better with time . . . I must wait for God to perform a miracle . . ."

We fill our souls with so many lies that eventually we lose the ability to see what is real and true about ourselves.

This cycle repeats itself over and over again, becoming a never-ending mantra of lies and deception, because the truth is so painful that we refuse to face it.

When we deceive others, we are simply exposing what is true inside of us. We are spilling out our soulish lies into the world and expecting that everyone will believe them as much as we do. We maintain our lies even though the truth would be so much easier to manage. But we have lost touch with the truth.

Until someone comes along and pulls us back from the brink of total devastation and destruction, we stick with our daily routine of refusing to see what is real and true about our lives.

We placate

In our desire to make things right, calm things down, or maintain the status quo, we offer up little pieces of ourselves as sacrifices to a "god of comfort" because we have become comfortable in the most uncomfortable reality we could ever imagine. We can't even see how awful it is, so we do what we must to maintain it. If someone tells us we drink too much, we appease him or her with a gesture of having only one drink a day or no drinks for a month. If a drinker tells us that we are the reason that his or her drinking has gotten so bad, we offer more effort, a cleaner house, more sex, fewer demands, or anything we can think of to pacify the situation. We placate so that we don't have to do anything else. We surrender ourselves one bit at a time rather than making a bold move that would transform our souls and our situation.

We are walking tranquilizers. We have learned every trick in the book to pacify the agitated and mollify the belligerent. We're willing to take just a little bit of hell so that all hell won't break loose. We appease the controllers by surrendering more control, trying harder and doing everything we can to reduce the tension and calm the storm so that everything will return to the sick normal to which we have become accustomed. We are the ultimate pacifists: don't fight, don't react, don't be who you are. Instead, back off, run away, close down, tell lies, deny reality, or keep quiet so that the latest crisis will die down and we can get it under control.

We cover

We are the world's most accomplished makeup artists. We have learned to cover the worst wounds with the most effective superficial treatment that will hide our pain and bury anything that needs to be changed. In honor of Adam and Eve, we've gone into the "fig leaf" business. If something pops up to the surface, we cover it immediately so that no one feels the need to intervene and help us. If we are ignored, we cover our pain with busy preoccupation. If we are insulted, we cover our pain with sick humor. If we are blamed, we cover our shame with distraction or deflection. We come up with countless excuses to cover the real reasons why we can't function or why the person we love can't show up to a gathering.

We have learned to cover the worst wounds with the most effective superficial treatment that will hide our pain and bury anything that needs to be changed.

Whenever we need to conceal where we have been emotionally battered and bruised, we put a leaf over it, hoping that no one can see under it or around the edges. But of course people do see, and we've learned to add another fig leaf, or a fig leaf extender. Our motto has become "Cover at all costs," but the biggest cost is the loss of our freedom, identity, self-respect, and even our very souls.

We never stop adding fig leaves. Eventually, we place them over our eyes as well, so we can't see beyond our pain and suffering. We don't see the truth about our situation, and we don't see what's happening with other people. Our obsession with covering up the truth extinguishes any interest we might have in others and makes it impossible for us to connect with their pain. We have enough pain of our own. As Helen Keller reportedly once said, "The only thing worse than being blind is having sight but no vision." Covering up has the effect of shrouding our lives in total darkness.

We enable

Enabling is such a classic symptom of dependency that to mention it seems trite, but it is no less true and every bit as powerful. Enabling can be described as doing all the wrong things for all the right reasons. At first, we allow things to happen because we don't know what else to do. We're confused and we want to be accepted, so we learn how to go along with others. We might join everyone in a drink, or watch porn, or become what someone else wants us to be, or do what someone else wants us to do to meet an unrealistic or unhealthy expectation.

When we look the other way, we enable really horrible things to happen. We allow the worst to happen when we try to rationalize why a bad situation might be fine in some way or another. We believe that our motives are pure, and we become experts at manufacturing excuses.

"The person has to want help before he or she will get help."

"There is nothing I can do."

"Aren't I supposed to submit to my husband?"

"I've tried everything."

We don't get help for ourselves. We don't go online to see that others have called an interventionist in impossible situations. We refuse to acknowledge that there are groups of people all over the world who have the same problem or are married to someone with the same problem. We don't look for those groups because we are committed to doing everything just as we've always done it, even though the same old patterns have done nothing but intensify our frustration at all levels. We've simply learned to live with it. We say that we would do anything to make our lives better, but in the end we do nothing.

We control

Why be a lowly doormat, getting stepped on all the time, when we can become highly respected controllers of all things? Some of us have learned to excel in this coping strategy. We didn't necessarily set out to become controllers, and we may not have seen it was happening; but as the problem got worse, we transformed our approach. At first, we were disappointed by what our loved one did or didn't do.

We were speechless, powerless, and hopeless. But then we turned our disappointment into a destiny. The other person's problem gave us a reason for being.

The worse the other person became, the better we looked. The more we had to sacrifice, the more we were praised by others for all we had to endure. The worse the problem became, the more respect we received. We began to thrive on the sympathy of others. We tuned our ears to hear how great we were in the midst of such failure and disappointment. We took charge of everything—planning our work and working our plan. We used every ounce of power and strength we had, but we felt secure because we were in control.

Sadly, many of us developed our own addictions, compulsions, habits, and dependencies because it isn't easy coping alone and trying to run another person's life while also trying to run our own. We learned to boost our efficiency with stimulants or stimulating relationships, and we comforted ourselves with alcohol, medication, or fantasy—anything that would take us away from the drudgery of reality for a while. We were able to control everything except the intensifying pain and increasingly damaging consequences of our actions. We reached a point where we were in far over our heads, taking everything onto ourselves, trusting nothing to God, and feeling an enormously lonely desperation and hopelessness. We think that control works until we lose control and have no choice but to surrender to God, who has been there all along waiting for us to ask him for assistance.

We think that control works until we lose control and have no choice but to surrender to God.

We attack

With the face we show to the world, most people think we're quite nice. But back at home, there is a price to be paid for our dreams not coming true. And we make sure that whoever is causing us all this grief understands, in great detail, the extent of his or her defective way of life. At every opportunity we attack, criticizing everything that does not please us perfectly. We keep score, and every way in which the other person has ever let us down, every unmet expectation, is available as ammunition for our next attack. We destroy the other person with our words and our disappointment, and then we withdraw before he or she can respond. Like hit-and-run felons, we reverse gear and roll back over the person we hold responsible for our pain, just to make sure he or she feels it as intensely as we do. We are nice to the world, but at home our cruelty knows no bounds. Not everyone is like this, but many are headed in this direction.

We isolate

Don't stick around if you don't have to. That's the motto of the isolationist. People who fear abandonment will sometimes preemptively abandon the other person instead, either by moving out or by simply pulling away. Moving out might be the right thing to do if we're not safe, but if it moves us toward greater isolation, it is not a step in the right direction. Some of us have become so ashamed of our lives that we stop letting anyone else in. It is a survival technique we learned in order to stay in control or stay alive.

Sometimes our isolation from healthy relationships is the result of our being controlled by another person. We fall for this person's explanation that he or she is only trying to protect us. We soon find ourselves separated from the very people who care about us and could help us. But rather than go back and reconnect, we continue to run away from them and cut them off when they try to reach out to us. We are on our own, alone in our pain and isolated from anyone who could offer us a path to freedom. We become fearful and self-doubting because there is no longer anyone healthy who is putting anything good into our lives. Our lives become secretive and obsessive, covered up and alienated from others. We become afraid of being known.

"Well, if you really knew me, you may not like what you see."

In every sense, our lives have become completely unmanageable.

Learned Helplessness

Each of these behaviors and patterns is part of reactive living. They are not healthy responses that will move us toward healing. If anything, these unhealthy reactions move us further from hope and transformation. We developed these reactions as a means of staying alive. But now they simply keep us from living. Because they come so naturally to us, we may be unable to see (or may refuse to see) that these reactions are all we have left. Unless and until we start the process of restoration and healing, these reactive strategies are the only choices we have available.

Reactive living eventually puts us in a state of learned helplessness. We feel trapped and unable to consider any healthy options.

Reactive living eventually puts us in a state of learned helplessness. We feel trapped and unable to consider any healthy options. We reach a point where we are totally dependent on others to do for us whatever needs to be done. We are like children who need a caretaker to make decisions for us because we act as if we don't know what to do. And even if we know what to do, we're convinced that we're not *able* to do it.

Our final reaction is to live in hopelessness. When we believe that life is hopeless, our learned helplessness spurs us on to prove it every day. We set ourselves up for failure and aren't surprised when that's what we get. We continue to react out of shame and fear. We don't choose; we react. Our flawed reactions to our pain create more pain to react to.

The hope for breaking out of this cycle of learned helplessness is for life to become so bad that we sense a need to give it up and surrender to a different way of living. We start to realize that there has to be a better way. And after all we've done to defend our reactions, we start to move closer to allowing a power greater than ourselves to take control. That is our only hope—but it's a good hope.

5

THE ORIGINS OF REACTIVE LIVING

WE HAVE WORKED together as authors and coauthors of many books, and we have also edited three major Bible projects together. We have been friends through thick and thin, and we know each other and each other's families very well. We have helped each other through situations involving divorce, a child with addiction, and all sorts of other issues that arise when two people live in close relationship for almost forty years. We started a counseling center together and have spent hours and hours together on *New Life Live!*, answering thousands of calls. Through all of that, we thought we knew just about everything there was to know about each other. But as we met to discuss the intricacies of this book project and what we're trying to communicate here, we made a new discovery.

We both detached from our families at an early age. I (David) can point to the age of six. Most people don't even remember what they were doing when they were six, except for maybe having a birthday party or raising a pet. But I remember it well.

My parents had given me a red Sheaffer mechanical pencil for my sixth birthday, and they told me not to take it out of the house for fear I would lose it—which is exactly what happened when I took it to a friend's house to show him. When I told my mother that I had lost the pencil, I asked her not to tell my dad. I wanted to tell him myself when I was ready.

One day, when he erupted about something, in his rage he made a point of telling me that my mother had violated my confidence and told him about the lost pencil. From that point on, I remember withdrawing from any emotional investment with my family. It was as if I became an "emotional orphan."

I remember withdrawing from any emotional investment with my family. It was as if I became an "emotional orphan."

When I was sixteen, I gave my dad a red Sheaffer mechanical pencil for Christmas, thinking that the time when I had lost my birthday present ten years earlier had been important to him. But he never recognized the significance of that gift, which only deepened my feelings of alienation from him.

This father-wound was finally healed in my life when I was in my forties. Steve knew about it, but he had never heard me talk about such an early age of detachment from my family.

I (Steve) did the same thing around the age of thirteen, when I "moved out" emotionally from my family. This was more than a typical act of individuation or the establishment of a separate identity from my family. I had a growing sense about my family that we were five very different strangers living under the same roof. I was related to them by blood only.

The connection at home was so thin that I looked for connection, attachment, and belonging anywhere else I could find it. I never brought my friends to the house, but I spent hours at the home of my best friend, Cliff, who was being raised by a very loving and caring mother after the death of Cliff's father. In many ways, I felt more related to Cliff than my own brothers and more comfortable at Cliff's house than my own.

When I was in high school, I started dating a wonderful, steady girlfriend, who had an exciting and adventure-filled family life. She and I did a little television show together, and we became very close. I felt much more like a part of her family than my own, and I longed to be at her house and with her parents. It was all a reaction against the rigid rules in my own family and the absence of a meaningful connection at home. My father, who had been raised by a John Wayne–type Texan, did not understand how to connect with his family or that connecting was even a goal. My mother had a very difficult time dealing with the loss of her father, which had happened when I was very young. My reaction to their parenting was to detach myself and go it alone.

When David told me that he had felt like a stranger in his own home, that was exactly how I had felt for years, and yet we had never shared that with each other.

Though we both reacted to our home life growing up with the same detachment, these reactions developed along very different paths. My (Steve's) journey out of high school and into college left me searching for attachment and connection wherever I could find it—most often with a girlfriend. I felt incomplete if I wasn't dating someone. I ended up in a lot of superficial relationships, often getting involved sexually as a way of feeling that I was wanted and that I belonged to someone. I never saw it as reactive living. I saw it as a normal way of life that any young man would choose. But I didn't realize that it wasn't entirely a choice. I had become trapped, and essentially owned, by my reactive attachments to the family I didn't feel attached to.

I (David) dated a lot in high school, but I was seen as being very detached. I might date a girl once or twice, but that was all. Then I met Jan, and we got married a month after I turned twenty. It has been in the context of my marriage that I've had to work out my issues of living reactively. In a sense, Jan and I had to finish growing up together. We call the first ten years of our marriage "the great tribulation." It wasn't until after I began to receive mentoring from an older man that things took a turn for the better.

Reactive Living

Before we look more closely at the origins of reactive living, we want to clarify exactly what we are talking about. Reactive living takes many forms, but it is often rooted in the lack of healthy attachments from an early age, which typically occurs when we don't bond and attach properly with our parents or early caregivers.

Reactive living takes many forms, but it is often rooted in the lack of healthy attachments from an early age.

It isn't very comfortable being a reactive person. We are always on alert for the next slight, insult, or threat that will trigger a reaction from us. When we can go from experiencing a little nirvana one moment to unleashing a full rage the next, it's no wonder we just want to keep the peace. Reactive people are easily overcome or overtaken by deep emotions—not because we choose to be but because we have so many triggers that are pulled by the people closest to us.

When we're triggered, we don't take time to sort through our thoughts. We have a set of reactions all lined up and ready to gush forth. We have perfected our reactions, refining the aspects of our behavior that don't push back hard enough or are ineffective in getting the person who pulled our trigger to walk away. Rather than think through the consequences of anything we might say, we fire a barrage of words that will most likely hurt the other person and deflect the focus away from ourselves and the real problem. Without any consideration, a stream of internal thoughts comes pouring out onto the other person:

"You are the problem."

"You know nothing."

"You have no idea what you're talking about."

"You are so stupid."

"No wonder you're such a loser."

On and on we go, spewing thoughts that should never have been revealed, but there they are for everyone to hear and judge.

When triggered, we also fail to process our feelings. We don't know precisely what we're feeling, but it's not good. We lash out and fling our feelings as they arise:

"I hate you."

"You disgust me."

"I'm tired of listening to you."

"You make me miserable."

"I can't stand being near you."

It's what we feel, and we think we have the right to get it out there. But it's a sad form of adult bullying to use our feelings as a means to knock others down and push them away.

Reactive people play the game of life more like checkers than chess. We think one move at a time. If I react to your move, you'll react to mine. We don't think three or four moves ahead, as a chess player would, because we're reacting, not thinking or planning. We simply go with our first instinct, which is most likely defensiveness, projection, blame, and shame. And if that barrage is not enough force to punish the other person, we will continue to find new ways to bring him or her under control. Rarely do we see anything other than our right to defend and deflect. We are in survival mode, and like any wild animal, we attack when we feel endangered. But we don't realize that we've surrendered our humanity and our freedom.

Reacting Like a Baby

In 1987, psychologists Cindy Hazan and Phillip Shaver published the results of their study of how adults act, react, and respond in romantic relationships, based in part on John Bowlby's research with infants on attachment, separation, and loss.[1] Hazan and Shaver found interesting correlations to Bowlby's findings about the ways that babies acted, reacted, and responded with caregivers who cared for them, inconsistently cared for them, or neglected them. They concluded that, while not all romantic relationships are based on or produce these childlike characteristics, most do. We can examine these traits of romantic love to evaluate the health of our adult romantic relationships.

Do you feel safe in the arms of the person you love?

Babies calm down and relax, showing that they feel safe and secure, when their caregiver is in close proximity and responds to their needs and signs of delight. In a healthy romantic relationship, adults feel safe, have lower anxiety, and enjoy the experience of the one they love being close and responsive.

Some people have become so accustomed to being uncomfortable in their close relationships that they associate the feelings with belonging or attachment.

It seems obvious that there would be some parallels between healthy baby-to-caregiver relationships and healthy adult romantic relationships. But many people have not experienced either one; rather than feeling safe in the arms of their spouse, they may feel controlled, anxious, or even terrified. Some people feel these unsettling emotions while dating and yet move forward with the relationship anyway. This could be because of feelings of unworthiness or because they have become so accustomed to being uncomfortable in their close relationships that they associate the feelings with belonging or attachment.

When we can step back and see that we have entered into a relationship that is not calming or soothing, or when a relationship develops into something destructive, we come to understand that we are not free and that we have not made a free, objective choice of a partner who would be good for us. In reaction to earlier neglect or inconsistent attention, we may have been driven to seek the familiarity of an uncomfortable relationship or to attach ourselves to anyone who would have us.

Do you engage in enjoyable close, intimate bodily contact with the one you love?
Babies thrive on close, intimate bodily contact with their caregivers. In a healthy adult romantic relationship, people are drawn to each other and engage in close, intimate bodily contact such as holding hands, hugging, kissing, and cheek-to-cheek proximity.

In romantic relationships, we are drawn to bodily contact, and much of it arises from sexual attraction. But in a truly healthy romance, we are able to show restraint. If we are desperate, we may act on our urges and become sexually involved before marriage. But this makes it difficult to navigate the other aspects of the relationship in a healthy way. Often, premarital sex is a desperate attempt to force attachment on the other person. Sexual involvement can be a reaction to a fear of being alone and isolated, which may have its roots in our infancy. In our experience, couples who are highly sexually active before marriage often wind up not wanting close, intimate bodily contact at some point after marriage. Separate beds, separate bedrooms, separate houses, and eventually separation and divorce replace the desire to be close. If we were making free and healthy life decisions, we never would have made some of the choices we've made. But we were not operating in freedom. We were driven by early life events that skewed our attractions and attachments.

If sexual activity is the primary attachment or bond between two people, marriage will tend to nullify its impact over time, and the attraction will die. A healthy relationship may start with a love for close physical contact, but it must move beyond the purely physical to provide satisfaction and sustainability.

Do you feel a little insecure when the one you love is not near you or responsive to you?

Babies show signs of distress, suggesting insecurity, when their caregiver is either out of sight and inaccessible or else unresponsive to actions that indicate needs or enjoyment. Adults in romantic relationships love being together, and they find it unpleasant and feel insecure when the other person is not accessible.

Though it's normal to feel a little insecure when someone we love is away, because they are so much a part of us, in unhealthy relationships we may feel terrified.

Though it's normal to feel a little insecure when people we love are away, because they are so much a part of us, in unhealthy relationships we may feel terrified. We become afraid they may not return, or we fear what they might do while they are away. We may even be afraid of what we might do while separated. Another possible reaction is relief. The relationship may be so sick that we love our time apart more than our time together. We might react by leaving, taking off because we are so uneasy with being in close proximity to the person who is supposed to bring comfort, joy, and fulfillment.

Do you love sharing discoveries about yourself, the other person, and your world?

Babies seem to enjoy sharing discoveries such as new sounds or new objects with their caregivers. In healthy adult romantic relationships, both partners love to share discoveries about themselves and their world with the other person.

When our romantic relationships are not healthy, our fear of rejection, retaliation, or ridicule can cause us to go from openly sharing insights about ourselves and our relationship with each other to protecting ourselves, hiding, covering up, and becoming secretive. Alternatively, our loved one may know just what to say or do to draw us out and win us over, but once we have revealed ourselves, we see the flip side to his or her personality, and we find that we are not free to explore or express ourselves honestly.

In a healthy relationship, the whole world opens up to us because we have someone to share it with.

In a healthy relationship, the whole world opens up to us because we have someone to share it with. We love to travel, go antiquing, or go exploring because we enjoy discovering new things together. But relational dysfunction restricts our world and binds us to the old, the sad, and the other person's control.

Do you show a fascination and mutual preoccupation with the one you love?

Babies and caregivers play with each other's facial features and exhibit a mutual fascination and preoccupation with each other. Adults in healthy romantic relationships also do something similar.

Fascination is replaced by frustration when we are trapped in a sick relationship. What preoccupies us now is how quickly someone who once seemed to hang on every word we spoke gets hung up on almost anything we say or do. Once, it seemed we could do no wrong, but now we question, evaluate, and second-guess everything we do or intend to do. And we seldom seem to get it right. Partners who are weak and insecure feel the need to prove us wrong at every turn in order to show themselves that they still have power. But they don't. They've simply found a way to tap into our weakness and trap us in their prison. The irony is that we gave them the keys and helped them click the lock shut. Our sickness has entrapped us and convinced us that we don't deserve to have our own lives. But we need to take our lives back.

Do you engage in baby talk or have your own unique language with the one you love?
Babies and caregivers engage in baby talk. Healthily romantic adults also engage in baby talk.

In a healthy love relationship, grown adults have been known to use silly, sugary baby talk that only the couple themselves can understand. They may also have a common sense of humor, with inside jokes, winks, and nods that enhance the loving bond between them.

But when a relationship takes an unhealthy turn, one partner may take on the role of an angry, displeased, shaming, never-satisfied parent while the other person becomes like a child or servant who is less powerful than the abusive partner. The relationship becomes all about control, defensiveness, and shutting down, often flailing and flopping from one form of abuse or neglect to another.

If you find yourself in an unhealthy, abusive relationship as the weaker partner, you would be best advised to extract yourself as soon as possible. That doesn't mean immediate divorce. It means getting yourself (and any children) to a safe place and then working to get yourself strong and well. It may sound simple, but it rarely is. Instead of acting, moving forward, and getting better, we can easily get stuck in a pattern of reactive detachment in an effort to survive.

Adult Reactive Attachment

To more clearly define what reactive living looks like in adults, it may be helpful to draw some comparisons to a widely known but comparatively rare childhood condition known as reactive attachment disorder (RAD), which is typically found when a child has extremely insecure attachments from being raised in an institution or by neglectful or cruel parents. When RAD occurs and these typical scenarios are not the cause, the source of the disorder can be difficult to determine.

We know parents who have adopted children from China, Russia, or Korea, and the adopted children have been able to attach and bond into healthy family relationships. We have also seen many instances where the adoptive parents are baffled at every turn by children who seem to resist every movement toward them, rebel against every rule meant to help them, and exhibit bizarre behavior in reaction to healthy nurturing efforts. When these parents take their children to get help and are given a diagnosis of reactive attachment disorder, it can produce great relief to know that someone else understands the problem and that there is a treatment for it.

We trust you will find encouragement and hope in knowing that a reactive way of life is common, it has identifiable symptoms, and there is help available to treat it.

As we look at some parallels between RAD and adult reactive living, we trust you will find encouragement and hope in knowing that a reactive way of life is common, it has identifiable symptoms, and there is help available to treat it. Each subhead below will list some symptoms of RAD, and we will explain how these behaviors manifest themselves in adults who are caught up in reactive living.

Emotionally withdrawn behavior toward caregivers

Acting out is negative behavior that is obvious to everyone who sees it. Abuse, violence, affairs, drunkenness, conflict, yelling, breaking things, hitting, and bingeing all are reactive behaviors. They are choices that hurt people emotionally and sometimes physically. When a woman whose husband has been unemployed for six months tells him it's time to start looking for a job and he storms out the door, goes to the nearest bar, and gets drunk, he is obviously acting out—or we might say *reacting* out.

The opposite behavior, which includes many forms of emotional withdrawal, might accurately be reclassified as *reacting in*. Rather than overt conduct that knocks other people back on their heels, *reacting in* is a silent withdrawal from connection and attachment, back into ourselves and away from others. We lose our ability to trust, or we have such anxiety in proximity to other people (often those closest to us) that we mentally and emotionally "move out," even though we may not actually go anywhere. This emotional detachment can be subtle and is often seen only in hindsight. We may not be aware of the drift, but looking back, we can often pinpoint a time when we felt as if we had moved as close as possible to the other person before choosing to move on—though, again, only internally. Building walls of resentment is often a construction project we undertake to protect ourselves. Passive-aggressive interactions—that is, saying the right things but doing something else to sabotage the other person's efforts—are also common.

When we stop seeking comfort from our closest relationships, we find other ways to comfort ourselves. We eat, drink, fantasize, view, seek out, consume, or use anything we can latch onto for some relief from our misery. When efforts are made to reach out to us, help us, and comfort us, we resist at every turn. We either don't respond or turn away. We appear not to enjoy or desire any kind of attention. Our unspoken message is fairly clear: *Go away.*

Chances are we don't even know what we're doing. We're just surviving by doing what we think anyone would do who has been treated the way we have been. We're not out to hurt anyone else or destroy ourselves. But by cutting ourselves off from other people, we break the link between ourselves and the healthy nurturing of our souls that we so desperately need.

We soon discover, however, that withdrawing from the battlefield doesn't keep us from getting hurt. So we redouble our efforts, perhaps trying to curl up into a smaller ball. Our walls grow thicker, our resentments deeper, and our detachments wider. More and more, we live inside our heads: dreaming and scheming, plotting and planning, spinning our obsessions as we gradually take back any emotional investment we've made in the relationship.

By cutting ourselves off from other people, we break the link between ourselves and the healthy nurturing of our souls that we so desperately need.

My (Steve's) wife, Misty, works with women who are waking up to their need for healing, recovery, and a new way of life. More than once, she has encountered a woman who wanted to remain single and never wanted children but now finds herself with a husband and four kids, feeling trapped with no way out. These women may start to *react in* with fantasies, or *react out* through online affairs, or even physical affairs. When they seek help, they come to understand that being single would have produced the same feelings of emptiness and longing that they are experiencing now. Their desired scenario may not have been a good option. Withdrawing, isolating, and acting in are also not good options. They have to face the truth of their devastation from past wounds and initiate the process of taking their lives back by discovering healthy and healing relationships with healthy and healing people.

Persistent social and emotional problems

Regulating our emotions is an adult behavior that some of us do better than others. In some ways, this difficult skill marks a boundary between teenage behavior and full adulthood. Both of us have raised teenagers and have seen the extreme emotional responses of adolescence go flying through the house, causing everyone a little—or a lot—of discomfort. It can be exciting, but also extremely draining, to do our duty as parents and help our teens rein in the unruly feelings that can take them down a path of immature alienation. But if teens don't learn how to regulate and modulate their emotions, the social consequences are disruption, destructive behavior, and sometimes even death from desperate acts.

This disruptive pattern is repeated in adulthood when we react in and stop responding to others. We become very adept at not giving others the satisfaction of our response. If someone is kind to us, we look away. If someone is uncaring, we act as if it's normal. We don't react outwardly toward others, but we react within, further burying our healthy emotions. People may say we are aloof and detached, but they have no idea how attached we are to an internal world that we've created for ourselves.

What others might see in us is unwarranted irritability. We may be fuming on the inside, but we're not going to let that be seen—until we lose control. Until then, our mild irritation or prickliness is only the simmering edge of a lava flow of anger that we hold inside. With the bland or noncommittal face we often turn to the world, no one could know the depths of our dark depression and hopelessness. We would be happy to experience the little bit of sadness we might show on the outside, rather than drowning in the well of despair we carry within us. And if we reveal our uneasiness or anxiety at being close to someone, it is merely the blunted edge of our fear that we'll be abused, neglected, or ignored as we've been before. We don't want others to see how afraid we are because they might tear down everything we have created for our own protection. So we hide as much as we can, and we deny any evidence that we are not ourselves.

Persistent lack of having emotional needs met by caregivers
This is how we've learned to roll. We go to the bar, surf the Internet, or seek out anyplace other than home to have our needs met. If we are stuck at home, we use busyness, clutter, eating, drinking, or anything else we can find to numb or stimulate ourselves. But our needs are never met, and we've stopped trying to have them met in healthy

ways. Just like the baby in the orphanage who stops crying and no longer asks for assistance or recognition, we gave up long ago. People look at us and think we are self-sufficient. Our outward system of orderliness covers the chaos on the inside and makes it appear as if all our needs are being met. But we're not going to let other people disappoint us again by showing them a need and having them walk away from it or use it against us.

Limited opportunity to form stable and secure attachments
In this respect, adults with reactive attachment issues are not unlike children reared in an orphanage, who have limited opportunities to form healthy attachments because there are no healthy people around with whom to bond. We all have many opportunities. Support groups and recovery groups are everywhere. Amazingly helpful counselors and therapists are practicing everywhere. If we look, we can't miss them. Couples therapy and intensive workshops to build intimacy are there for us to experience, but we don't. Any of these resources would turn us around so we could form secure attachments. But as we react, we destroy stability. As we run from healthy responses, we intensify our insecurity. As we react in, we refuse to seek help that would promote healing and establish healthy bonds, which would meet our ongoing needs and lead us toward fulfillment.

Responding to Reactive Living

If we react to our reactivity, it only gets worse, and we become more and more miserable. *Responding* rather than reacting is the option we want to move toward. The proper response to our crippling condition is to seek out the safe and stable living conditions that we missed in our earlier years. Typically, we don't know how to do that, so we need a guide or a sponsor to assist us. That could be a therapist, a counselor, or a knowing pastor who could help us find what we need.

If we forgive ourselves and others, we can replace our bitterness with some positive interactions.

For some people, getting to safety is the first response they need help with. If we are reacting in order to protect ourselves, we need an environment safe enough that we don't feel a constant need for vigilance and self-protection. We need help finding new places that stimulate our creativity and give us new focal points beyond our internal miserable selves. We need consistency and continuity that will allow us to explore what it's like to be ourselves with others, absent of any shame or blame as we stumble toward becoming responsible adults. We have a lot more to say about this in Part II: The Responsive Life.

If we forgive ourselves and others, we can replace our bitterness with some positive interactions.

Reactive attachment disorder is a clinical diagnosis for a child. Adult reactive attachment disorder is not an official, clinical diagnosis. It is a way of life. It is how we have come to process life, and it has left us wanting and unfulfilled. Hope comes from seeing the problem, wanting something different, and being willing to do whatever it takes to heal and meet the unfulfilled needs of our lives. If you'll stay with us, we will help you make the astounding transition from reactive living to responsive living.

6

SURVIVING BROKEN ATTACHMENTS

GOD DID NOT design human beings to live reactive lives. He wired us to connect with other people. We don't do well when we are reacting in or reacting out. An illustration of this basic need to connect can be seen in a newborn baby's brain, which has about 200 billion nerve cells. But by the time the child reaches five years of age, that number has been reduced to about 100 billion nerve cells. And that's normal.

What happened to the other half? As the child grows and experiences a variety of events, circumstances, and people, nerve cells in the brain are connected to other nerve cells. Those that connect survive. The half that fail to connect will die. Don't feel bad; it's part of God's design. He determined that about 100 billion nerve cells is the right number for an adult brain. This "wired to connect" principle applies to life in general, as well. When we don't connect with other people, a part of what makes us healthy human beings also begins to die.

In the previous chapter, as you read about various types of unhealthy family environments, you may have wondered why anyone would be loyal to such dysfunctional people. But because we are wired to connect, we must find some way to bond with other people when we are growing up, even though it may be an unhealthy, dysfunctional, or insecure attachment. Regardless of what our family of origin was like, we all needed to connect in some way, even though some of us were forced to adapt or limit our connections because of our internal pain.

Even in the best of families, the attachment between parent and child is freighted with the anxiety, fear, and uncertainty of both people.

If you were raised in a family that made healthy connections difficult, you already know that your parents' anger, fear, shame, or anxiety made home a highly unsafe place. Even in the best of families, the attachment between parent and child is freighted with the anxiety, fear, and uncertainty of both people.

During the second half of the twentieth century, psychiatrist John Bowlby developed a theory of how children form relational attachments, especially with their parents. The prevailing theory at the time was focused on the child's inner world, but Bowlby believed that the real-world attachment between mother and child was more important than the child's inner world. His work laid the foundation for understanding both healthy and unhealthy attachment relationships.

In Bowlby's definition of a healthy mother-child relationship, the mothering person provides a stable base of operation for the child— a fortress in which the child feels safe and secure. Gradually, the child will feel safe enough to venture out from the fortress to explore other parts of the world. When a child begins to feel uncomfortable, anxious, or unsafe, he or she is able to return to this protected base and enjoy safety and security once again.

Bowlby developed his ideas in part by watching mothers and

toddlers in the parks of London, where he saw several different patterns of behavior emerge. Some toddlers, when taken out of the stroller, would hang around Mom for a while and then go off and play. The mother would interact with the other moms, but she also kept an eye on her toddler. Occasionally, the toddler would check in visually with the mother to make sure she was still there. Sometimes the child would even come back to the mother to get a hug, or simply a touch, from her. This pattern characterized what Bowlby called a *secure attachment*. The toddler expressed and experienced a measure of freedom and independence, but always within the safe and secure realm of relationship with the mother.

Bowlby also noticed a second relational pattern between some mothers and toddlers. These toddlers, once freed from the stroller, would go off to play, either alone or with friends. But in this relationship, the child never came back to the mother, and seldom even looked at her, until she called out that it was time to leave the park. These toddlers seemed indifferent toward their mothers, and the mothers seemed indifferent toward these children. A mother would occasionally check to see where her child was, but most of the time she was deeply engaged in conversation with other mothers. These children seemed secure, but they also seemed to know that the mother was primarily interested in her friends. It wasn't necessarily neglect, but it was a lack of attentiveness to the child. Bowlby referred to this type of self-sufficient mother-child interaction as *anxiously avoidant attachment*.

In a third type of interaction between mothers and toddlers, the child would hang around the mom, never going very far away. This child also tended to be clingy and would intrude on the mother's conversations. At the same time, the mother didn't want her child to go too far away. In some cases, it even seemed as if the mother needed the child to be close more than the child needed the closeness. It was as if she derived some protection from the child. Bowlby referred to this type of mother-child connection as *anxiously ambivalent attachment.*

Further research done by developmental psychologist Mary Ainsworth and others identified a fourth type of insecure attachment—one built on a foundation of fear rather than anxiety. In one observation of a mother and son in Ainsworth's experiment, the boy moved toward his mother with arms outstretched—a normal part of a mother-child reunion. But midway through his movement toward the mother, the child stopped, turned around, and backed into her. Ainsworth later found that this child had been physically abused. In the pending reunion, he didn't know whether he would be hugged or hit. His style of connection was a *fearful attachment.*

Let's look at each of these early attachment styles, how they express themselves in adults, and how they lead to classic codependency.

Insecure Attachment: Avoidant

We'll begin with the second relational pattern—anxiously avoidant attachment—to see how it manifests in adult relationships. At first it might appear that codependency wouldn't be part of an avoidant adult's experience. After all, he or she is thought to be self-sufficient. But the appearance of self-sufficiency is a symptom of anxious attachment. Typically, adults who learned to attach this way were raised by an anxious mother, and their needs, as children, were not that important to her.

An attuned mother will know when her child is hungry or tired and will respond accordingly. An avoidant mother doesn't adjust to the child's pace.

Mothers of anxiously avoidant children are often preoccupied with themselves. In their relationships with their children, they can range from being mean to simply being cool and detached. Though the degree of detachment will vary, the common denominator is that the mother doesn't respond in an attuned way to her children's needs.

An attuned mother will know when her child is hungry or tired and will respond accordingly. An avoidant mother will eventually get around to meeting the child's needs, but she doesn't adjust to the child's pace, even when the child is an infant.

Eventually, children raised this way will figure out that they're on their own. But they aren't happy about that internally. Some will express their anger through random acts of aggression. They may become bullies later in childhood or even in adulthood. As adults, they often blame others for anything that goes wrong. As children and as adults, they become adept at using lies to worm their way out of responsibility.

Another example of avoidant attachment is the shy loner, who may seem almost emotionless outside the home. As adults, some are content to have their primary relationship be with their computer, while others will have one or two friends at the most but won't spend a lot of time with either one. When they marry, they basically shut down emotionally. A spouse may spend a lifetime trying to get a shy loner to come out of hiding, but that only makes the loner feel more unsafe and want to stay in hiding. The majority of children with avoidant attachments will grow into this type of adult.

A third type of avoidant attachment results in adults who are more severely wounded by the neglect and abuse of their parents. These children escape reality by daydreaming a lot, and they may have trouble functioning normally as adults. They show little interest in the real world and may still be financially dependent on their parents well into adulthood. In the home, they may allow their anxiety to show by being clingy and demanding. They struggle with trust issues and believe that everyone will be as unreliable as their parents were when it comes to meeting their needs. It is difficult for children to feel accepted when their parents are unavailable and unresponsive, and these deficiencies carry over into adulthood.

Adults with avoidant attachments can easily get caught up in codependent behavioral patterns. Because they have essentially taken care of raising themselves, they may exhibit unhealthy levels of narcissism. This often shows itself in compulsive perfectionism, which they probably developed as children in an effort to gain their parents' approval or capture their attention. When that failed, they may have decided to help others do things perfectly—which comes across as very controlling. In addition, they are cut off from their emotions, and they may be uncomfortable with physical touch.

Adults with avoidant attachments can easily get caught up in codependent behavioral patterns. This often shows itself in compulsive perfectionism.

Simmering beneath their perfectionistic tendencies is a deep anger over what they didn't get during childhood. They may not even be aware of their anger, but others certainly are. We can imagine how their codependency developed: If they can give what they didn't get, maybe they'll get the love and approval they long for. They do this by taking care of others.

Like every other codependent, those with avoidant attachments have had to bury their real self. Because they didn't get the nurture and attention they needed, they grew up thinking that there must be something wrong with them. This is a common theme with all insecurely attached adults, but those with avoidant attachments conceal their insecurity with an air of self-sufficiency.

Insecure Attachment: Ambivalent

Adults who grew up with ambivalent attachments have absorbed their parents' ambivalence and anxiety. As infants, they tended to cry a lot and to be very clingy and demanding, both at home and away from home. Their anxiety is rooted in the fear that they will be abandoned—first by their parents and then by their spouse and even their children. They are also very angry, but they typically control their anger because it would otherwise negate any chance for solace and connection. When the mother is away for some good reason, the child feels abandoned and protests the separation with tears. When the mother returns, the child is angry but quickly becomes clingy and even babyish in his or her reactions.

Parents of this type of child are ambivalent about their role as parents. Sometimes they are there for the child; other times they are emotionally or physically absent. Children raised in ambivalent homes often wonder how their parents—particularly the mother but also the father—feel about them: "Do they even love me?" They have a continual feeling of abandonment, or impending abandonment.

The parents' anxious ambivalence is transferred to the children as they grow. The children are often impulsive, tense, unable to fully concentrate, and easily upset by failure. Other characteristics include hypersensitivity to life's difficulties, a failure to take initiative, and a tendency to give up too easily on difficult tasks. The parents may or may not be available and may or may not be responsive. And because the unpredictability of the parents' attention causes anxiety, there is little chance that children from an ambivalent home will feel accepted.

When these children become adults, they often exhibit a high degree of pain, along with a haunting sense of separation that is sad to observe—and even sadder to experience. They struggle with feeling unworthy of love and with feelings of incompetence. They are especially frustrated by a sense of being incapable of getting the love they need and want. They struggle with the fear of being left alone or rejected.

As adults, these children almost universally become *pleasers*. But they are ambivalent pleasers. Sometimes they try to please; other times they give up, feeling that they can't even do that right. After all, that was their experience as children. Sometimes they tried to take care of their parents; other times they weren't even noticed by their parents.

Typically, those with ambivalent attachments are still dependent as adults on one or both of their parents. At the same time, they are in the midst of an ongoing, angry, emotional war with their parents. Often, they have tried so hard to get their parents' approval that they stay enmeshed with them, still hoping for what they never got as children. When they marry, they may expand the emotional war to include their spouse. But because they so desperately want to avoid being abandoned, they cannot maintain their warlike posture, or else they might force their parents or spouse to leave, resulting in actual abandonment. Neither can they pretend to be self-sufficient, for that may also drive people away. So they try to please everyone, with the hope that they may finally feel loved and accepted.

By burying their real self—because they believe it is the cause of their pain—and working hard to create a false self that will finally earn the love and respect they desire, adults with ambivalent attachments epitomize classic codependency. But all that effort never works! We can't fix internal problems with external solutions.

Insecure Attachment: Anxious

Though all insecure attachment styles are rooted in anxiety, there is a form of attachment that is especially anxious. Adults with anxious attachments often come from homes in which the parent-child roles were reversed and the child became the responsible "parent" to their irresponsible, chronically ill, or incompetent parent. As a result, these children were robbed of their own childhoods. They feel anger, but it is often expressed passively because they fear rejection if they were to reveal their true feelings.

Anxious attachments occur when the parents themselves are extremely anxious and fearful about life— especially when they are anxious about parenthood.

Anxious attachments occur when the parents themselves are extremely anxious and fearful about life—especially when they are anxious about parenthood. Some become "helicopter parents," transferring their own anxiety about the world to their children. These parents' anxiety may be a result of the ungrieved death of a loved one or the chronic illness of one of their own parents. Whatever it is that undermines the normal parenting role, the child becomes an emotional or physical caretaker for the obviously needy parent.

This reversal of roles only adds anxiety to the child's life. Children are unprepared emotionally for the responsibility of caring for their parent's needs. As they have to parent the parent, they become an extension of the parent and forfeit their childhood in the process.

As adults, people with anxious attachments become the self-appointed caretakers of the world. After all, that's how they were raised! They tend to marry irresponsible or needy people, such as alcoholics or other kinds of addicts. Even when they vow not to repeat the pattern, they have an unconscious need to have someone to take care of.

Underneath their caretaking behavior is an anger that can be punishing at times. They are good at being encouraging and positive, but these traits only go so deep before these people run into the anger and humiliation they feel. They are comfortable in adult relationships or careers only when they can be the parent. They are simply too accustomed to being in control.

Insecure Attachment: Fearful

Another subset of insecure attachments is one in which the child becomes fearful of connection because of abuse. When a mother is physically abusive, her children never know whether she is going to show them love or punish them. That creates tremendous confusion and fear. Sometimes the abuse occurs because the mother doesn't know how to protect her children from someone else who is abusing them. She feels inadequate, helpless, and out of control, and she may lose control over the children, as well, because they can no longer trust her for safety and stability. Sadly, many adults who grew up with fearful attachments pass along that fear to the next generation, often through the very same kinds of abuse they suffered as children. Taking your life back entails breaking dysfunctional patterns and cycles and forging healthy relationships with healthy people.

Moving toward Forgiveness

All people who have insecure attachments blame themselves for their anxiety and insecurity. They are convinced that their real self is bad or worthless; therefore, they feel undeserving of love, affirmation, and positive attention. That's a painful reality, so they learn to bury their real self and create false selves that they hope will eventually earn them the love, respect, and connection they long for. They often do this by finding people they can take care of. Codependency is alive and well when one needy person meets another.

Adults with insecure attachments may struggle with the impact that their parents have had on their lives. But that doesn't mean the situation is hopeless. Insecure attitudes toward our parents tend to take one of two paths. Some people believe that we should never say anything negative about our parents. This viewpoint is often expressed in words such as these: "My parents may not have been perfect, but they did the best they could." It's true that we should be grateful that our parents took as much care of us as they did, but that's no reason not to deal constructively with their shortcomings and the effects they had on us. And it's better than the other common attitude, which is unrelenting anger, bitterness, and blame for all of the problems they caused us. But truthfully, neither attitude is helpful in taking your life back.

Forgiveness means we cancel a debt that can never be repaid— which is the only possible resolution for an unpayable debt.

Instead, we need to remember and understand what happened,

place and accept responsibility where it belongs, grieve what was lost in our childhood, protect ourselves from repetitive hurtful behaviors, and ultimately forgive our parents. Forgiveness means we cancel a debt that can never be repaid—the only possible resolution for an unpayable debt, as I (David) explain in detail in my book *Forgiving What You'll Never Forget*.

Just as important as recognizing where and how we were wounded, we must also be able to identify our own attachment issues. Remember, "you can't heal a wound by saying it's not there!"[1] As you've been reading, we hope you've been able to identify and come to grips with the insecure attachments that may have dominated your growing-up years and may still be at work in your adult life. In Part II, we'll discuss what to do about them.

What about Secure Attachments?

The mother of a securely attached child has provided a safe and stable base from which the child can venture out to explore without anxiety. When the child begins to feel anxious, he or she can return to the predictable safety and security of the mother. Securely attached children feel confident that their mother will be available, caring, and nurturing. Children may cry when the mother leaves, but they are always happy when the mother returns. They also willingly allow the mother to comfort them when she returns.

We cannot have a secure connection unless both people—child and parent, or husband and wife—are *available*. A parent can be too available, as in the case of helicopter parents or controlling parents, or too unavailable, as we've seen with rejecting or neglectful parents. But God designed parenting so that all a parent has to do is be "good enough." One key for determining what is good enough can be seen when parents and children reunite after a period of separation. How do both the parent and the child handle the relationship when the parent returns? If there is a healthy attachment, they will have a comforting and cheerful reunion.

Children who are raised with secure attachments are also able to express their negative emotions constructively. They may cry, shout, or pout, but they know they will get a meaningful response from the parent. These negative emotions will not make the child feel all-bad; nor will they cause the parent to become defensive. Instead, such behaviors are simply curtailed by the parent without characterizing the child as bad or evil. Secure parents are not threatened by a child's negative behavior, and they are able to express their negative emotions to the child in appropriate ways. When parents and children have a secure attachment, the parents will be *responsive* to the child.

When my (David's) mother-in-law was a child, it was not unusual for her father to create turmoil at the dinner table. He would make a noise, such as a grunt, and the others at the table would suddenly be in a panic trying to figure out what he wanted. If they didn't figure it out quickly enough—say, that he wanted the butter—he would become enraged but still would not say what he wanted. He was available—that is, he was physically present—but he was not responsive. For whatever reason, he was unwilling to simply ask for what he wanted. Availability and responsiveness must go hand in hand.

All three elements—availability, responsiveness, and acceptance— are necessary to form healthy, secure attachments.

Acceptance is the third leg on the tripod that creates safety and security in a relationship. How the parents handle their own negative emotions, as well as their ability to respond positively to the child's frustrations and negativity, goes a long way toward making the child feel accepted.

All three elements—availability, responsiveness, and acceptance— are necessary to form healthy, secure attachments. Because no parent does it perfectly and no child is able to do it perfectly, even the best attachments won't be perfect. And it's impossible to avoid being wounded to some degree by these imperfections. That's simply the human condition in a fallen world. So even with secure attachments, we will struggle in some way with the issues we've discussed, especially with feeling accepted.

Growing up with secure attachments does not guarantee that all our adult relationships will be healthy, or that we won't be codependent (though secondary dependence is more common than classic dependence when a person comes from a healthy background). And it doesn't mean that we're in touch with our real self (though the search may be a shorter process). Regardless of our background or the quality of our attachments, finding our real self and taking our life back involves pursuing adult relationships that are based on healthy and secure attachments. And even in the best of situations, we may still struggle to some degree with the issue of toxic shame. Let's now turn our attention to that important topic.

7

SHAME ON ME

At 12:04 a.m. on March 24, 1989, an oil tanker bound for Long Beach, California, from Valdez, Alaska, struck Bligh Reef in Prince William Sound, spilling more than 11 million gallons of crude oil into the water and onto the surrounding coastline. The *Exxon Valdez* spill is still considered one of the most devastating human-caused environmental disasters in history. The effects of the spill, including some sickening images of wildlife covered in oil, can still be viewed online.

As I (Steve) was watching a video of some rescue workers cleaning up a large bird that was completely covered in black sludge, in my mind's eye I saw a picture of my former self at a time when my life was saturated with shame. At one point, I had become so aware of my mistakes and failures that it was as if I were slathered with the ugly black sludge of shame, to the point that it had become my identity.

Shame is pervasive like that. We don't just feel it; we wear it. And it's ugly. If we bring it under control enough to cover it up from others, we only intensify its impact exponentially. Our shame-filled secrets can make us sick and can even become deadly. Whenever I hear of a male suicide, I wonder whether it was caused in part by sexually generated shame. Sometimes, when a man is caught or exposed in sexual sin, the shame of facing a future in which other people know what he has done can be unimaginable. But whether it is through gradual deterioration or a sudden end, secret shame is toxic enough to kill us.

Reacting to Shame

Not all shame is bad, but toxic shame is a reaction that defines and destroys us by causing increasing devastation as it flourishes and begins to overtake more and more of our lives. We have a friend who became a stripper after losing a baby about four months into her pregnancy. Although she had been raised as a Christian, she was estranged from her parents and was living with her boyfriend at the time of the pregnancy. It took the loss of the baby for the shame to set in. But her feelings of shame did not cause her to return to a life more consistent with her values. Instead, she ran in the opposite direction, straight into a lifestyle that would own her for several years before she finally woke up to what she was doing. Shame took her hostage, pulling her deeper into sin and away from the person that, deep down inside, she really wanted to be. Mistakes piled upon more mistakes until she became convinced that she was a defective person unworthy of anything good.

Toxic shame undermines our will and our power to stand up for ourselves.

Toxic shame undermines our will and our power to stand up for ourselves. Often, when we talk to abused spouses, they describe feeling like second-class citizens—or even third- or fourth-class. In their shame, they had a sense that from the very beginning they were somehow lesser than other people and deserved nothing but the crumbs of life. They had settled into destructive relationships as if that were their destiny. So when the abuse continued, they felt as if they deserved the horrific treatment. Their reaction to toxic shame was to accept being mistreated, blame themselves for being mistreated, and continue to tolerate the mistreatment rather than seeking help and finding hope.

Toxic shame carves out a new normal for those who partake of its poisonous fruit. Rather than seeing themselves as human beings who have made a few mistakes—maybe even some really big mistakes—people who are saturated with toxic shame see their failures as an objective expression of who they are. Before long, they don't even try to avoid future mistakes. They don't learn from their errors because they don't think they can, or need to, learn anything. Repeated mistakes are simply a self-fulfilling prophecy that their shame has written for them. Mistake management is their normal role in life because they feel as if they themselves are a mistake.

We've all had times when a few poorly conceived actions came crashing back on our heads, and the difficulties they caused may have been quite extreme. But most of us waded through the wreckage, cleaned up the mess, and got back on track after learning a hard lesson or two. Toxic shame, on the other hand, blinds us to wisdom and insight. It prevents us from cleaning up after ourselves. We start to live in the debris of past mistakes, and that leads us to more debris-producing decisions. We fill our lives with problem after problem because we don't think we can do any better. We believe we are destined to make all things worse. In our minds we see ourselves as a worst-case scenario creating more worst-case outcomes from a deep well of toxic shame. That shame has etched into our hearts a self-image of a person living under the rubble of inevitable, disgraceful errors at every turn in life.

Toxic shame turns us away from goodness. Anyone who looks good or does good things will cause us to reject him or her immediately. We view anyone who tries to reach out to us in our toxic shame as a "hypocritical do-gooder" who must have some ulterior motive beyond just wanting to help us. We shun them before they can shun us. The last thing we would ever want to do is change ourselves to be more like these "losers" who have it all together. Rather than seeing healthy people as potential role models or mentors, we want to roll over them or run the other way.

Toxic shame turns us away from goodness. We reject anyone who looks good or does good things.

We believe that these people whom we judge and criticize have nothing to teach us because we don't think that learning anything new will take us to a higher level. Our shame has convinced us that we're stuck right where we are and that nothing we can do can take away the self-loathing we feel deep in our bones. We don't think meaningful change is possible. Not after what we've done. Toxic shame is our new reality, and we refuse to live a lie by pretending that anything good can come of our situation.

When we succumb to toxic shame, we react to our pain and futility with quick fixes and instant solutions that don't accomplish anything. Our actions become compulsive, or we dive further into addiction as we strive to find relief for the pain. Our obsessive thoughts and recriminations torment us night and day. Our compulsions drive us from one repetitive source of damage to another. We don't need God or anyone else to punish us because our shame is punishment enough. We live as if our souls were covered with a black, poisonous sludge, and that sludge will kill us if we don't allow something outside of ourselves to remove it, in much the same way that rescue workers cleaned up the contaminated coastline, ocean, and wildlife after the *Exxon Valdez* covered the pristine arctic world with gobs of black.

The shame cycle

In 1997, I (Steve) wrote a book with Connie Neal called *The Emotional Freedom Workbook*. In that book, we created a cycle that shows where toxic shame can lead us.[1]

THE SHAME CYCLE

As this cycle continues, we spiral downward into a state of ever-increasing rejection, isolation, and sickness. Toxic shame continues to breed more and more poison, which then leads to more and deeper feelings of shame. But there is another way.

Another Kind of Shame

As bad as shame can be, and as poisonous as our reactions to it can become, there is such a thing as *good* shame. A better term for it might be *godly sorrow*. No matter what we call it, good shame has some distinct characteristics that separate it from the soul-killing black sludge that our lives produce in reaction to sickening, secretive shame. Responding to godly sorrow makes our lives better and moves us into closer alignment with every good and perfect aspect of God's purpose and plan for us.

Godly sorrow is a warning sign that we are on the wrong path and need to make some adjustments. Any mistakes we make are seen not as the inevitable result of who we are but as stark reminders that—because of who we are, created in the image of God—we can do better. We are genuinely sorry that we fell short, hurt ourselves or other people, or simply created a lot of hassle that has kept us from living in the good things that God has for us. However, our defective behavior is rightly seen as separate from our identity. Making a mistake doesn't mean that *we* are a mistake; it's simply evidence that we are like every other human being—completely capable of many things, including mistakes.

When we are in a right frame of mind and when someone does something abusive or neglectful to us, we can immediately recognize that we can do better and that we deserve better, and we can take steps to avoid any abusive situation where someone might try to take advantage of us. Bad behavior against us is not seen as punishment for past mistakes or as something we deserve. We don't punish ourselves when we do something harmful, and we don't punish ourselves when we experience something great, either. We respond to our world as we encounter it, believing that we are no better and no worse than other people. We feel no need and see no reason to inflict ourselves with more pain, struggle, and difficulty.

Godly sorrow is a prompt from God, and from a well-developed conscience, that we need something more to achieve all that we want to accomplish. We respond to healthy shame with a desire to get better or do better; we don't react to our shame by trying to preserve our self-image at the expense of our self-respect. And we certainly don't make matters worse by compounding one mistake with another. We protect ourselves from repeated mistakes by avoiding people and places that set us up for failure or expose us to needless temptation, abuse, or neglect.

Godly sorrow is a prompt from God, and from a well-developed conscience, that we need something more to achieve all that we want to accomplish.

When we experience shame, our healthy response is to feel it as godly sorrow: a temporary but powerful emotion that points us to something that needs to be changed as soon as possible. We do not adapt to living with shame or make more room in our lives for godly sorrow. Instead, we focus our energy on positive and healthy responses, corrections, and even restitution, if we have wronged someone. When we respond appropriately, we expect to move forward without being defined by or hindered by the murky sludge of toxic shame. We know the things that lead us to higher ground and a better life, and we move toward them even when it is difficult or seems impossible. As we continue to move in a positive and healthy direction, we will notice that our feelings of shame are reduced by our responsible behavior.

As we continue to grow, we begin to see how shame can be a very valuable tool to guide us and keep us out of trouble. When we stumble, we repent, receive God's forgiveness, and forgive ourselves; but we don't minimize the damage of the past and set ourselves up for future failure by taking forgiveness for granted and neglecting all the things we have learned and done to strengthen our recovery and protect ourselves from harm. When we get in trouble, the flashing lights of godly sorrow warn us that we are flirting with disaster before we dive headfirst into it. Now when that horrible feeling of shame comes over us, we see it as a protector and safeguard of all that God has invested in us.

When feelings of shame begin to surge within us, we have permission to withdraw and regroup. We withdraw to evaluate what lies ahead and who is involved. We don't recklessly rush into situations or relationships that may harm us. We are not out of control. We have a new power of discernment that alerts us to the danger of our shame becoming toxic if we don't pull back, evaluate our situation, and protect our recovery.

We no longer feel the need to create a crisis in order to be noticed. We are secure in who we are. We don't have to get involved in bad things just to feel that we're part of something. We are aware that God has a better way for us if we will surrender to him every day.

Shame that we convert to godly sorrow becomes a trusted friend, keeping us on the right track, where God wants us to be.

In Part II, we will show you how to break the cycle of shame. But we want to end this chapter with a few more observations about the harmfulness of shame-based living.

Shameful Conclusions

Toxic shame is a mind-set that we want you to eliminate from your life. It may have been foisted upon you, or you may have picked it up on your own. What's important is that you understand that how you deal with shame is a decision you must make if you want to take your life back. Poisonous shame can be self-ingested when we believe the lies we're told by others and the lies we tell ourselves. We need to renew our minds with God's truth.

How you deal with shame is a decision you must make if you want to take your life back.

Here is a quote from one of the first people to receive a *Life Recovery Bible* when it was published in 1998: "I stopped believing the lies of Satan and started believing the truth of Jesus Christ, and it changed everything."

I (Steve) never expected to hear those words come out of her mouth, and I doubt that she ever would have thought she'd be quoted saying something positive about Jesus. For some people, even hearing the name of Jesus is offensive because of Christians who don't act as Jesus would act. They draw a lot of attention, while many faithful servants who just want to help others are often overlooked.

I met this woman at a meeting set up by Chuck Smith Jr. of Calvary Chapel. She was at a suicidal crossroads. This was a shame-filled, drug-addicted, child-neglecting mother, whose life was continuing to spiral downward. Chuck felt that he had not been able to help her, but he handed her the *Life Recovery Bible* as she left, suggesting that she start reading with the book of John.

Six months later, when I preached at Calvary Chapel, this woman was almost unrecognizable. She had taken her shame-saturated soul and had replaced all the lies that sentenced her to an early death with the truth about the abundant life available through Jesus. Not only had she turned her own life around, but she also was already helping other women get their lives together. Going from helplessness to helping others is a testimony to the power of replacing shameful lies with God's truth.

If you are stuck on lies about yourself, you are inflicting toxic shame on yourself. And you don't have to do that. You can't just stop the lies, however. You have to replace them with truth. The *Life Recovery Bible* is an excellent resource to help you do that. If you are bearing shameful lies from another person or from many people, you need to stop repeating the lies and start answering them with truth, such as the words that Jeremiah repeated from God in Jeremiah 29:11: "For I know the plans I have for you. . . . They are plans for good and not for disaster, to give you a future and a hope." That is truth you can take to the bank. You don't have to remain stuck in shame. You can choose to step into a life of promise that is anchored in God's redemptive and unchanging truth.

If you cling to your shame, you will stay disconnected and isolated, involved in harmful relationships and sabotaging any chance of getting help. The lingering fallout will be a growing bitterness and a seething rage: what you believe to be the most justifiable resentment anyone has ever known. You will hold on to your grudges, and when you can no longer contain the boiling tempest within your soul, you will lash out, destroying other people at random and looking for all the world as if you are out of your right mind. And in fact, you *are* out of your right mind, because a mind that is set right is full of God's love, truth, grace, and peace and of a deep sense of belonging. To live in your right mind, you must get rid of all the destructive shame that is left.

There is a better way to live than being fearfully insecure and reacting to every minor threat that comes your way.

There is a better way to live than being fearfully insecure and reacting to every minor threat that comes your way. Your readiness to react is part of what prevents you from taking your life back. You spend all your time defending your dysfunction rather than taking a risk and creating something entirely different, positive, and better. You are dying in a pool of toxic shame. You are stagnant, sick, and missing out on the exhilarating feeling of God's grace blossoming in your life.

Healthy living is optional. Taking your life back is optional. You make the choice. You can continue to live in the shadow of unrealistic and unmet expectations—either the ones you think that God has for you, the ones that others put on you, or the ones you craft for yourself—and you will continue to live in the sludge of toxic shame. Or you can keep reading and find the pathway out of shame and the keys for taking your life back. We challenge you to break the hold that shame has on your life. You can take your life back, and we will show you how.

8

THE IMPACT
OF TRAUMA

SOME STATEMENTS ARE obvious yet need to be said anyway, just so we don't miss the point. Here's an example: *Trauma causes people to do things they never would have done if the trauma hadn't happened.*

Obvious, right? But we've chosen to highlight it here in the hopes that it will break through, soak in, and become a factor in your ongoing journey to take your life back, find God's truth, and live accordingly.

During high school, I (Steve) made a staggering transition from being a pretty good guy who had made a few mistakes to being a very destructive person, both to myself and to others. I betrayed the people I cared for the most, and I ran away from the people who cared the most about me. I acted out compulsively and exhibited all sorts of addictive behaviors. I piled one mistake on top of another and wound up as a very messed-up young man, full of shame and with disconnected and superficial relationships. I was on a path that eventually led to an unplanned pregnancy, which I made worse by pressuring my girlfriend to have an abortion. That decision led to male postabortion syndrome, which at the time I had never heard of but which left me full of toxic shame and overwhelming regret.

Through the course of all this trauma, I eventually made the decision to accept God's forgiveness for all I had done, forgive myself, and take my life back.

I eventually made the decision to accept God's forgiveness for all I had done, forgive myself, and take my life back.

For years, when I looked back at my younger days, I hung my head in regret. I was amazed that, at a time when I had so much going for me and was so blessed in so many ways, I would veer off the path of righteousness and have no desire to get back on it. I would describe myself as the worst of the worst because no one had abused me and no one had driven me to do anything wrong. In my arrogance, I had taken control of my own life—and then had driven it into the ditch. I had disregarded the counsel of others and messed up everything that was good and wonderful in my life, causing tremendous pain to some other people along the way.

Even after I came to terms with my shame and accepted God's grace and forgiveness during a prolonged process to take my life back, it was always a mystery to me how it all could have gone downhill so quickly. At one point, it felt almost as if I had gone off to war and suffered a traumatic battlefield injury, coming home a different and damaged person; but there was no war, I wasn't a soldier, and I had suffered no injury. But the change in my life had been that dramatic.

When attention deficit disorder (ADD) began to be explored and defined in the 1980s, I thought it might be an explanation for some of my struggles. A few years ago, I went to see Dr. Daniel

Amen at the Amen Clinic in Southern California, where they had identified seven types of ADD. There they took a brain scan to determine which type, if any, I might have. I figured if they could diagnose the problem, I could better understand how to deal with it and make the best of it.

After the scan, Dr. Amen told me he didn't like what he had seen on the scan. I thought maybe he had identified an eighth type of ADD, perhaps a terminal form, and that I would be the first person ever to die from TADD—terminal attention deficit disorder. Things like that are always occurring to me . . . because I have ADD.

But that's not what Dr. Amen told me. He asked me whether I had ever suffered a significant brain trauma. The answer was no. Then he asked about automobile accidents. I remembered a rainy day when my father and I had driven to the dealership to trade in his year-old Pontiac for a brand-new one. (My dad bought a new car every year.) About three blocks from the dealership, we were at a red light when a man plowed into the rear of our car. I've had neck problems ever since because of whiplash from that accident, but that didn't explain what Dr. Amen had seen on my CT scan.

Then he asked me about football, which I had played from seventh to twelfth grade. I was a center on the offensive line for many of those years, and then I played fullback, where I would run the ball and block for other players. Dr. Amen said that football was the most likely explanation for why my prefrontal cortex projected a flat image on the CT scan, rather than the oval shape that would be expected. And it was also the most likely explanation for why certain structures in my brain that should have appeared rounded like marshmallows looked more like flattened pancakes.

The center in football is kind of an anonymous player, but he is also one of the most likely to receive a head injury because the concentration required to snap the ball to the quarterback leaves the center more vulnerable to an undefended hit. In the era when I played football, the helmets were designed to prevent skull fractures, not brain injuries. On top of that, I really wasn't very good. So, when I was hit by an opposing player, it was not unlikely that my brain would have crashed against my skull. I would have taken the full force of the hit, and the other player would have experienced little resistance from me.

I took the diagnosis from Dr. Amen and had a further examination of my brain function by psychologist Rick Tansey, who operates a brainwave optimization program called Max My Brain. They hooked me up to some electrodes and recorded my brain-wave activity in the form of electrical currents. The results of the study were that the left side of my brain was about eight times hotter than the right side. Rick Tansey said it was "on fire." You might think that a lot of activity would be a good thing, but those parts of my brain were so active that in a sense they were paralyzed. When challenged, those parts shut down and I could not respond. This finding, combined with the brain scans taken by Dr. Amen, were fairly conclusive: My brain had suffered some type of trauma.

The evidence for some sort of trauma was real and compelling, and it made more sense out of my past and present decisions than anything else I had seen.

For the first time, I began to reflect on my last year of playing football, and I remembered feeling as if I had really gotten beaten up. When I compared my off-field behavior before my last season of football with my behavior after that season, it made sense that something had traumatized my brain. It helped me to understand how I could have seen such a dramatic change in my choices. Yes, I was a typical teenager at the time, prone to impulsive decisions and not thinking things through entirely. And yes, as a normal human, I was capable of messing up my life without needing any other factors to blame. But the evidence for some sort of trauma was real and compelling, and it made more sense out of my past and present decisions than anything else I had seen.

Various Types of Trauma

Trauma occurs when an extremely stressful event destroys our sense of security, leaves us vulnerable, and maybe even reduces us to a state of helplessness. If you have been traumatized, you know what it feels like to be overwhelmed, to obsess about when the next dreaded catastrophic event might occur or about when you might be abandoned. You know what it's like to wait for the next insult or threat of physical harm, or to be lied to in a way that makes you question your sanity. Some of us have lived this way for years and have depleted every emotional or psychological reserve we ever had.

When we are traumatized, events happen unexpectedly, and we find ourselves unprepared to handle the shocking reality or horrific threat that we face. We shrink into believing that we are powerless to prevent further trauma, and we try to rid our minds of the memories of what occurred in previous episodes. When we have repeatedly been traumatized by a cruel or indifferent person or by difficult or uncontrollable circumstances, and when this string of traumatic events dates all the way back to childhood, it is easy to see the damage that can be done. Even just one traumatic event can have a tremendous and lasting impact on our lives.

The traumas we see most often in counseling are caused by sexual, physical, or verbal abuse, including domestic violence and neglect. We also see bullying and gaslighting—a deceptive technique for controlling a relationship in which a person tries to distort and define reality for someone else. When we are repeatedly or continually coerced, manipulated, or put down, it's easy to see how life could start to seem impossible and how we could feel helpless, hopeless, and overwhelmed.

If you are wondering whether your own experience would be

considered traumatic, here are some symptoms that often surface as a result of trauma:

» Muscle spasms, tension, and sharp pain
» Aches and pains in your organs, bones, and skin
» Fatigue, waking up tired, and never gaining energy throughout the day
» Being jumpy or easily startled
» Being constantly on edge or alert, and being upset by seemingly small things
» Racing or irregular heartbeat
» Sleep disturbances, including nightmares, insomnia, and frequent and early awakenings

All of these physical symptoms accompany reactive living, as well. Most trauma survivors live reactively and may also see psychological symptoms emerge:

» Withdrawal from others in an attempt to stay safe
» Feeling disconnected from God, others, and even reality
» Numbness that makes it difficult to respond quickly to stimulus
» Paralyzing shock that hinders normal, open reactions
» Complete disconnection and withdrawal from others
» Toxic shame, unrelenting guilt, and obsessive regret
» Inability to concentrate or focus; difficulty in making simple decisions
» Feeling confused or even crazy
» Compulsive, self-protective behaviors, such as lying, secrecy, or making excuses
» Depressive thoughts of hopelessness and extreme sadness
» Emotional augmentation resulting in the extremes of shame, regret, rage, and excessive irritability

The Trauma Bond

One of the most unlikely results of trauma caused by another person is that we may form a bond with the perpetrator. Even though the person is toxic and unsafe, he or she exudes power and strength, which we may be drawn to. So we may cling to an abuser and return for more ill treatment rather than run for the door. If people ask us why we are so loyal to someone who is so cruel, it is very likely that we have become part of a trauma bond. Even when trauma is the primary feature of a relationship, we may stay attached to an abusive person who uses excitement, fear, sexual aggression, extreme behaviors, and risky situations to force us to cling and bond.

In reactive living, our reaction to a trauma-inducing individual is not a conscious choice. It feels like the only choice.

In reactive living, our reaction to a trauma-inducing individual is not a conscious choice. It feels like the *only* choice. We may feel foolish making this choice, but our fear wins out, and the bond continues. The longer this sick relationship lasts, the more devastating the consequences will be.

At the time we started working together, there was little talk in the mental health field about the impact of trauma on dysfunctional relationships. The focus was primarily on the role of the enabling codependent, who was often viewed as sicker than the trauma-inflicting individual. Fortunately, someone finally noticed that these enabling or supportive behaviors were more complex than simple choices. In fact, these behaviors were not choices at all; they were predictable reactions to difficult people and predicaments.

What is not so different between enablers and trauma victims is that they both need help—and the sooner the better. And the right kind of help is available. There is no bias against enabling or dependency issues. We have a much more complete understanding of trauma and its effects on decision making. People who have been robbed of their freedom are treated with compassion and without judgment. We know why they may have put so much effort into concealing everything and trying to live invisibly. For anyone who has been traumatized, the help available today is far more compassionate and understanding than it was even five years ago.

If you have been hit hard by trauma, we hope you understand that it's possible to change the way you are reacting to it. We hope you will be able to reach out and find new strength and resources. Then you can move on rather than remain trapped by the trauma that has kept you locked away from the life of freedom and joy that you could be living.

9

THE LOSS OF
YOUR REAL SELF

AT THE BEGINNING of this book, we looked at how the older brother in the parable of the prodigal son developed ineffective ways of dealing with his woundedness—through detachment, judgment, and bitterness. And we've seen how we can develop the same ineffective strategies for dealing with our own childhood woundedness, which includes our early attachment styles and the effects of shame and trauma.

Codependent behaviors have become pervasive in our society. According to the National Center for Health Statistics, "about 43 percent of US adults have been exposed to alcoholism or problem drinking in the family."[1] Add to those numbers all the people dealing with sexual addictions (including pornography) and drug addictions (including prescription drugs), and the circle widens to include just about all of us. And let's not forget that codependency itself is a form of addiction, one that takes a great toll on lives. It affects the hormonal balance in our brains, affects our bodies through chronic and terminal illnesses, shuts down our emotions, attacks our soul and our spirit, and undermines our relationship with God.

Dependency Issues and the Human Brain

When we ingest a chemical, such as alcohol or a drug, we spark a response in the pleasure/reward center of the brain. All drugs of abuse, from nicotine to heroin to alcohol, cause a particularly powerful surge of dopamine in the nucleus accumbens, the part of the brain that neuroscientists refer to as the pleasure center. That part of the brain is also associated with the compulsive processes that eventually lead to addiction.

Not every addiction is related to dopamine or the nucleus accumbens. Codependency and other process addictions may operate with adrenaline as the primary hormone. Codependency also taps into the limbic system, which involves our appetites and our emotional responses, such as fear and anger. In other words, codependency doesn't tap into the pleasure center; it is more fear based or anger based. There is no pleasure gained by being codependent.

Why are most dependency issues based primarily on fear? Think of how they develop. Starting with insecure attachment issues and adding the effects of shame, trauma, and woundedness, we can understand why a developing child wouldn't feel very safe or secure. The task of ensuring our safety starts in the amygdala, a little almond-shaped collection of neurons buried deep in the brain that integrates our emotions and our motivations. Its primary task is to warn us of impending danger. The amygdala signals the release of adrenaline and other hormones to prepare the body for the fight, flight, or freeze response. In dysfunctional homes, the amygdala is repeatedly stimulated, and neural pathways related to high stress and fear are formed. Eventually, these response patterns become automatic.

When we bury our real self, we become hypersensitive to anything that appears to threaten our security—not just our physical security but also our emotional security. As soon as anything triggers the feeling of being unsafe, we get a shot of adrenaline without even realizing it. The unsafe feeling could be as basic as picking up on a depressed mood in another person. This can result in constant vigilance, as we monitor our reaction to the other person's behavior. When we live in someone else's territory, we are forever on alert lest we miss an important cue and fail at our codependent task.

When we bury our real self, we become hypersensitive to anything that appears to threaten our security—not just our physical security but also our emotional security.

Growing up in a highly stressful environment pits the two sides of the brain—the emotional side and the logical side—against each other. When we're forced to live with fear, especially of being abandoned or rejected in some way, or when we're forced to repress our anger to avoid making things worse, we gradually turn off the reasoning part of our brain because the way we're being treated makes no logical sense. Eventually, we stop trying to understand.

As we repress our faculties of logic and struggle on with our emotions, the emotional part of the brain gets stronger and eventually takes over. Over time, as we are forced to learn how to read the moods and emotions of our parents, we become quite skilled at sensing emotional danger in other people. Unfortunately, we don't develop the ability to read our own emotions and moods. We're too busy watching for danger. All we're aware of in ourselves is our fear, along with an undercurrent of anger.

By the time we become dependency-based adults, all of these processes are automatic. Without thinking, we just follow the well-worn and heavily traveled neural pathways in our brains. It's kind of like a trail in the woods that leads from the general store to a cabin you've rented for the week. The well-traveled pathway to the store may be the long way around, but it's probably the path you'll take without even thinking about it.

Changing our automatic responses involves creating new neural pathways—which, to extend our example of the cabin in the woods, may involve hacking around in the brush and the forest a little bit. But one day, as you're taking the long way to the store, you realize that a shortcut is possible but there's no trail for it. So you get a machete and cut a new path. It may take a lot of effort, but eventually you clear a better way. Still, it's not yet automatic. You have to keep taking the path and keep clearing the underbrush.

Next year, when you rent the same cabin, you're surprised to find that your new pathway looks very inviting and well-worn. As others have used it, the path has become stronger and clearer. The old pathway is still there, but because it's not used as much, it's no longer as clear or obvious.

Taking your life back requires time and repetition. You're "blazing" new and healthier response patterns.

For our brains to recover from their childhood patterning, new neural pathways must be established. That's why taking your life back requires time and repetition—you're "blazing" new and healthier response patterns. We'll look at how to do that in our discussion of the responsive life in Part II.

Dependency and the Body

Stress is a natural consequence of living with fear and anxiety. One researcher likened it to a runner preparing for a hundred-yard dash who gets stuck in "get set" mode.[2] When sprinters prepare for a race, they may jump around a bit to warm up before setting their feet on the starting blocks. When the starter says, "On your mark," the runners shift into their starting stance. When the starter says, "Get set," every muscle tightens as the runners anticipate exploding out of the starting blocks. But what if the starter never fires the gun?

The runners are left in the starting blocks with adrenaline coursing through their bodies. If they stay in "get set" mode for very long, they will soon collapse.

The researcher's point is that we live in a "get set" world. Our fears and anxiety never let up. This is especially true for codependents, who are constantly "reading the tea leaves" in their relationships.

For years, depression was thought to be caused by a chemical imbalance in the brain. Pharmaceutical companies have spent countless millions designing targeted medications to deal with shortages of neurotransmitters such as serotonin. But other research suggests that the chemical imbalances are a *result* of depression rather than a cause.[3] Chronic and continually high stress causes the brain to change hormonally, increasing both adrenaline and cortisol. An excess of these hormones leads the brain to change in other ways, as well. For example, the hippocampus, which is related to short-term memory, may shrink, causing us to become more forgetful.

In addition, the executive part of the brain—the prefrontal cortex—also shrinks. That's the part of the brain we use when making decisions, and it's where long-term memory is stored. Shrinkage can be caused by too much adrenaline and cortisol in the system. Cortisol, the stress hormone, is designed to have a short-term purpose. Through exercise and a good night's sleep, it dissipates from the body until it is needed again. But when we live with high stress and depression, we often don't exercise properly or get enough sleep, which can leave residual amounts of cortisol in our system. The double-whammy is that the effects of high stress can make it more difficult for us to make the life changes that are necessary to reduce our stress.

All of that, in turn, weakens our immune system. We begin with small complaints, such as "I'm tired a lot" or "I ache." Eventually these complaints can become illnesses such as gastritis or high blood pressure, or they may even lead to serious physical debilities such as chronic fatigue syndrome. A compromised immune system limits our ability to fight off infections and can contribute to the effects of terminal diseases such as cancer or heart disease. Most illnesses that send us to the doctor are stress related in some way.[4] We aren't meant to live like this. Our bodies can't handle chronic stress. But Life Recovery is the antidote.

Dependency and the Emotions

Repressing our emotions also weakens our immune system—which doesn't bode well for adults who are dependent and who operate on the unspoken rule that it's not okay to talk about or openly express our feelings. For those of us who buried our emotions a long time ago, repression is an easy rule to follow. We may have become quite adept at reading the emotions and moods of others, but we've lost touch with our own emotions.

Unfortunately, in burying our negative emotions, we tend to bury all of our emotions.

In repressing our emotions, we're trying to bury only our negative feelings. We don't want to deal with the pain, but we still want to experience the positive emotions of love, joy, and peace. Unfortunately, in burying our negative emotions, we tend to bury *all* of our emotions. As a consequence, we can't risk being too happy or joyful because digging out those positive emotions may bring us into contact with other buried but painful emotions. In seeking to feel joy, we may end up feeling pain that we're trying to avoid. The sudden shifts from joy to pain can be confusing. But it's all because our emotions are connected to each other. What we do with one emotion, we tend to do with all our emotions.

Unexpressed anger can lead to sudden, inappropriate outbursts that go way beyond what might be anticipated. If we buried our anger in childhood because our parents were unavailable, unresponsive, unaccepting of us, or abusive in some other way, we can end up projecting that anger onto our spouse, kids, boss, or coworkers—often out of proportion to what's going on at the time.

In many cases, we turn that anger against ourselves, which contributes to our depression, compulsive behaviors, and addictions. Unexpressed anger doesn't dissipate; it just simmers under the surface. Others can often sense it more than we can. We think it's buried—and it may be—but it's only an inch under the surface.

Unexpressed fear may result in anxiety disorders, insomnia, heart arrhythmias, and sexual dysfunction. Unexpressed guilt and shame may lead to self-neglect, weight issues, and other compulsive or self-destructive behaviors. It may cause us to shame, blame, or criticize other people in our lives. Passive-aggressive behaviors are a common response to repressed emotions.

Unexpressed feelings also negatively affect our immune system, making us vulnerable to all sorts of illnesses. Feelings and emotions are not limited to the mind; they affect every part of our lives—physical, relational, and spiritual.

Dependency and Our Soul

The obvious foundation of our spiritual journey is our relationship with God. But which self do we bring to that relationship? Which self do we bring to *any* of our relationships? If we have kept our real self buried, how can we bring it into our relationship with God? Maybe that's why codependents struggle so much in their relationship with God. We try to play it safe by showing God a false version of ourselves. Fearing that our real self is just too damaged,

If the only self we bring into our relationships is a false self, we will end up with shallow, disappointing, and predictable relationships.

we don't want to be truly known, not even by God. But if the only self we bring into our relationships is a false self, we will end up with shallow, disappointing, and predictable relationships.

What we usually end up with is a God shaped in the image of our parents and friends. This kind of God may feel safe, but our relationship with him will always fall short of the reality of who God is and who he meant for us to be.

There is a scene in C. S. Lewis's *The Lion, the Witch, and the Wardrobe* in which Susan asks Mr. Beaver about Aslan the lion, who is a Jesus figure in the story.

"Is he—quite safe?"

"Safe?" Mr. Beaver replies. "Who said anything about safe? 'Course he isn't safe. But he's good. He's the King, I tell you."[5]

Lewis is pointing to the fact that God is unpredictable and beyond our control. God does what he wants, when he wants. But we can still completely trust him. Whatever he wants for us will be good because God himself is completely good, completely faithful, and completely trustworthy.

So Aslan's "unsafeness" is different from what we mean when we describe other people—our parents or others—as unsafe. Their unsafeness is based on their being predictably *untrustworthy*. We may think they are good, but we cannot always rely on them to do what is best for us in every situation. Consequently, there is a limit to how open and honest we can be with them.

When I (David) dealt with my codependency issues, I realized that I had been working really hard over the years to build my relationship with God. I went to Bible college, got involved in different programs there, and ended up leading a parachurch youth ministry where my salary was based on donations. And it seemed to me that God was just like my own father—always a day late and a dollar short. (I remember one time when I had to pay a bill by a certain date, but there was no money available for my salary. The funds arrived after the bill's due date—a day late.) I worked as a pastor for almost twelve years, all the time hoping it would increase my intimate connection with God.

Unfortunately, I was trying to bring a false self into my relationship with God during this time. I didn't realize it; all I knew was that I was frustrated and angry with God because he didn't seem to act the way the Bible portrayed him. I was aware to some degree that all my relationships were off-kilter because unknowingly I was trying to relate to people through my supposedly pain-free false self.

It was only when I was able to face the pain of my childhood and bring that pain into my relationship with God that I could begin to relate to God through my real self. And much to my surprise, my other close relationships—with my wife and sons—changed as well. God finally became not a simple extension of my natural father but instead the ultimate Father I found represented in the Bible.

With any dependency, it's never going to work to try to fix something on the inside by doing something on the outside.

I had vowed to myself that I would be a different father to my boys than my father had been to me. But I found out that vows don't work—or at least, they don't work for long. With any dependency, it's never going to work to try to fix something on the inside by doing something on the outside. Healing can only come from the inside out, and that means we have to rediscover and uncover our real self. After all, God made our real self; we're the ones who tried to make our false selves. The false selves may work in some situations, but they always fall short.

Your journey to take your life back will involve getting beyond your false self and breaking free from fear, anger, and shame so that you can bring your real self out of hiding. We've seen how taking your life back will affect your brain, your body, your emotions, and your relationships, especially your relationship with God. But before we can begin the healing journey, we need to look more closely at how it affects your soul.

10

LOSING TOUCH WITH YOUR SOUL

THE DIFFICULTIES DESCRIBED thus far have cost us all something. But the greatest price we've paid is the loss of who we really are. We have lost touch with our own souls. When we consider all the fallout from trauma, attachment issues, inhumane family rules, and the wounds of abuse, it's no wonder we feel unworthy. And with all that pain inside, it's no wonder we try to resolve our internal issues by making adjustments to our external world. Getting close to the pain simply hurts too much.

What does it look like to lose touch with one's soul? It varies. Take Bob, for example. When he decided to become a medical doctor, his family was excited. *How special*, they thought, *to have a doctor in the family*. But then, they expected nothing less.

Very early in life, Bob had learned that any attempt he made to achieve academic success made him a hero in his parents' eyes. With his 4.0 GPA all the way through middle school, high school, and college (and all the accolades that went along with it), getting accepted at his number-one choice of medical schools—Harvard—was just the icing on the cake.

If there was an honor to be achieved in med school, he achieved it. After all, he couldn't stop now. He continued to excel in his residency and soon built a very successful private practice. Everything he put his mind to, he accomplished. To any observer, he had it made. But all his success was on the outside. In his heart, he secretly struggled with feelings of being an imposter. He lived with the haunting fear that he would someday be exposed as a fraud. Though he tried to push these thoughts out of his mind, he couldn't do so unless he medicated himself with alcohol.

There was no life-altering trauma, no deep early wounding in his childhood—just a sense that he was valued only for what he accomplished. That was the unspoken family rule. And once all his accomplishments finally lost their luster, his internal world began to fall apart, even though to all outward appearances his life was a major success story. Feelings of fear, self-loathing, and shame became so overwhelming that he finally had to look for help.

In his recovery, he acknowledged that he had always struggled with feelings of inadequacy. And he finally realized that it was because everything in his family was based on performance. Love and approval were meted out in proportion to what he was able to do or accomplish.

When he was young, he had pushed through those feelings and accomplished more. But now he realized that his early decision to become a doctor wasn't based on being called to that profession—it was simply a way to get attention and approval from others. Because it all looked so good on the outside, no one ever would have thought that Bob had a deep-seated need to be valued just for being himself—just for being here.

Mary's story is quite different. She was raised by a codependent mother and an alcoholic father. Her childhood bedroom was next to the laundry room, and she remembered all the times she'd been awakened by the washing machine running in the middle of the night. The first time she checked to see why her mother was doing laundry at such an odd hour, she got roped into the family secret.

In what proved to be an all-too-common occurrence, her father had come home drunk, climbed into bed, and immediately gotten sick. Mary's mother not only faithfully cleaned him up, put fresh pajamas on him, and changed the sheets, but she put the soiled sheets and bedclothes in the washing machine before going back to sleep.

One night, Mary's father didn't make it to the upstairs bedroom. When she woke up in the middle of the night to use the bathroom, she found him asleep on the floor, lying in his own vomit. Mary woke him up and cleaned him up before calling her mother to escort him upstairs. Then she proceeded to clean the bathroom and put her father's clothes in the washing machine before going back to sleep. It was an automatic response for someone in training to become an enabler when she got her own problem person to take care of. After college, she graduated to chief enabler when she married an active alcoholic. Her codependency made her very good at doing exactly what her mother had done.

Both Bob and Mary lost touch with their souls when they were young. They gave up their real selves and developed lives that revolved around taking care of or meeting the expectations of someone else. Ultimately, their efforts were failed attempts to win approval, acceptance, and love. Bob thought that if he achieved his goals, his family and others would fill the approval holes in his soul. Mary and her mother thought that things would get better and that they would feel the love they both desired if they just showed they cared enough.

The Problem with Ourselves

When we lose touch with our soul, we have really lost touch with our true self. We can blame it on our busyness, our lack of time for self-reflection, or even the excesses of our culture. But in truth, we have done it to ourselves. We have given in to fear and shame, and we have settled for living through the externals of life. The result is a lowered sense of self-worth, even though we try to augment our feelings by doing all kinds of things that seem like good ideas but end up only working on the outside. It's like rearranging the deck chairs on the *Titanic*, or making sure the outside of a cup is clean but not bothering to clean the inside.

When we lose touch with our soul, we have really lost touch with our true self. We have given in to fear and shame, and we have settled for living through the externals of life.

We don't typically express the problem in outward ways, such as comparing ourselves to someone else and feeling that we're not as smart, attractive, or popular. It may start that way when we're young, but as we mature and become more sophisticated in our self-loathing, we're more likely to turn inward with statements such as "I'm a damaged person" or "I feel worthless." These statements pinpoint the problem as internal, as something within ourselves. It isn't that we have bad relationships; it's that we are basically bad on the inside. And because it's an internal problem, nothing we do in the external world will even touch it. Feelings of emptiness just sit there on the inside and fester.

When we try to fix internal problems through external means, it not only doesn't help; it also leads to a place where we are truly out of sync with ourselves. Tragically, instead of changing strategies, we often just try harder to refine our false selves in hopes that we can finally get the formula right.

It's easy to see why that's an impossible task. Unless we clear out the shame we have accumulated, eliminate the bitterness and anger we have nursed, and face the fear that has hindered us, nothing will change. But that's where Life Recovery begins.

The Problem with Others

Until we free our real self from its burial place and bring it into alignment with God's design for our lives, being out of sync with ourselves will also put us out of sync in all our other relationships. One belief we must give up is the notion that we are being loving and caring when we act out our codependent behaviors. Codependent behavior is not based on or motivated by love. It is rooted in our need to feel accepted and needed. Codependence is a futile attempt to fill a hole inside ourselves, and it doesn't lead to close, healthy relationships.

As we regain awareness of our real self, we need to stop saying yes to everything and stop trying to manipulate situations so we don't have to say no.

As we regain awareness of our real self, we need to stop saying yes to everything and stop trying to manipulate situations so we don't have to say no. We're afraid to say no because we might disappoint someone. The truth is, we can't say a healthy no if we have weak or porous boundaries or if we've built walls to shut out other people. Healthy and safe attachments are possible only if we take responsibility for ourselves and stop blaming others.

When one of my (David's) kids began to confront an addiction, our family was required to be involved in the recovery program. This led my wife and me to join an ongoing group of other parents and addicts. I was used to running groups like this, but I wasn't used to participating in one led by someone else. But Jan and I joined the group.

It was an awkward introduction as the group welcomed us in. When I said, "I'm here because one of our kids has a problem," a young man who was dealing with alcoholism nearly jumped out of his seat as he said to me, "That's what's my dad said when he came the first time! You're going to find out that you're here because *you* have a problem!"

Fortunately, I didn't have to respond. Later, I understood what he meant, and we became good friends.

That conversation reminded me of a number of parents who came to counseling for help with one of their adult kids. One couple said, "Our son has problems," and when they listed a few, they included still living at home at age thirty-one; not having a job and not looking for one; and sleeping until noon while supposedly still trying to take some college courses. He also hung around with friends who smoked pot.

When I asked who supported their son, they said, "Oh, we do. He's got to have some spending money."

"Who pays for school?"

"Oh, we do."

I said, "It doesn't sound like your son has any problems. Life for him is pretty easy. He sleeps as late as he wants, and he doesn't have to earn a living. It seems more like you, the parents, have the problem." Every time I have a conversation like that with parents, I think back to the young man who insightfully told me the same thing about myself years ago.

Our goal in taking our lives back is to realign with our true self so we can develop healthy, loving, and open relationships in which we feel accepted and affirmed for who we are rather than for what we do. We will finally find the peace and serenity we long to experience when we develop relationships in which we truly care for one another.

The Problem with God

We have yet to meet a practicing dependent who has a healthy, vibrant relationship with God. How can we bring our false self into a real relationship with God, whose real self is his only self? We can't. When we lose touch with our soul, our true self, we suffer spiritually.

Finding our soul means we have to resurrect our real self. And that takes time and hard work. Life Recovery involves basing our lives on the acceptance we have in Jesus, not on our feelings or circumstances.

Perhaps you've been frustrated or angry about the distance you feel in your relationship with Jesus. Maybe it seems as if he hasn't heard your prayers or he's somehow avoiding you. A common false self that many Christians develop is a "spiritual false self," in which we act as if everything is going great in our relationship with God, even though we feel empty inside. But when we get alone with our thoughts, that's when we feel the disappointment and the distance between ourselves and Jesus. But Jesus sees through our false selves to the true self we've buried within us. He wants to help us rediscover and reconnect with our true self—the true self he designed and intends for us to live in.

Finding our soul means we have to resurrect our real self. And that takes time and hard work.

When we're honest enough to admit our powerlessness and submit ourselves fully to God, we discover that Jesus is our true, fully sufficient, and fully available power source. His power is perfected in our weakness.[1] But surrendering to our powerlessness means that we have to give up our false selves and recover our real self. That's all part of moving from a reactive life to a responsive life, as we'll see in Part II.

The Responsive Life

REINTRODUCTION

WE HAVE LOOKED at what causes and characterizes reactive living. Now it's time to consider the more desirable alternative—*responsive living*—and to explore how we can begin to *choose* to live that way. A simple way to describe the responsive life is that it's the opposite of the reactive life. But to be more specific, here are three characteristics that mark the distinction between the two ways of living.

We Learn to Act, Not React

Instead of reacting automatically out of our woundedness, we begin to see and believe that we have choices. Responses are not pre-programmed. We can look at a situation and decide how we are going to respond.

When my wife and I (David) began to *respond* rather than *react* to our son's addiction, we had to learn new ways of relating to him.

Instead of trying to avoid conflict by giving him whatever he asked for, we had to learn when and how to say no.

I remember a time when he was in dire straits, all because of his own actions. It wasn't easy saying no, but as a family we had learned that we had choices and that saying no was the right decision, even though it was painful. Instead of continuing to react to make the problem go away temporarily, we were now making responsible decisions based on long-term healing and recovery.

We Learn to Trust

One of the main characteristics of reactive living is that we've learned not to trust anyone because they were bound to disappoint us or we were bound to disappoint them. Typically, we learn this in our family of origin, especially when family loyalty is low or nonexistent.

One of the first tasks we encounter in our healing is developing a trusting relationship with someone. We're all aware that no one, including ourselves, is totally trustworthy. So the key is to find someone whom we already trust to some degree and to be prepared to do repair work when it seems as if trust has been broken. Building trust takes time, and it is always risky; but healing cannot be done in isolation. It requires connection building.

We must learn also to trust ourselves again, as that is the basis for making good decisions. Trusting ourselves goes hand in hand with building a trusting relationship with another person. And as we build trusting relationships on earth, we gradually learn how to trust God, as well.

We Learn to Feel

In navigating our dependent relationships, we have learned how to read the emotions of others. Unfortunately, it wasn't for the purpose of better understanding the other person; it was a matter of sheer survival. At the same time, we learned to bury our own feelings for the same reason—to survive. Our feelings don't ever go away, but they can become distorted and difficult to access. So now we must learn how to identify what it is that we're feeling.

The first strategy we use is hindsight—that is, identifying our emotions after the fact. As we reflect on a situation in which we went back to old patterns of behavior, we can try to identify what our emotions were at the time. Gradually, we learn how to identify our emotions as we experience them.

Sometimes, when we first tap into our emotions, they feel very negative and hurtful. That's because, as we begin to feel again, we may re-experience long-buried emotions that were painful. Don't let the pain become a deterrent to the process. Becoming a responsive person takes time. It won't happen overnight. But the time to begin is *now*.

11

TAKING YOUR
LIFE BACK

IMAGINE TAKING A soda straw and a bottle to Lake Tahoe and try-ing to drain a portion of it to create a piece of dry ground on which to build something solid. No one in his right mind would do that. But that's the equivalent of what we do when we drain ourselves in attempting to change someone else, in waiting for someone to wake up one day and decide to change, or in expecting God to swoop in and perform a particular miracle for which we've been praying.

It's a complete waste of time to put all our time and energy into something that we have no ability to change, improve, or even affect. When we take all that we have and waste it on someone or something that will return nothing in exchange for our efforts, we continue to live in reactive ways. Instead, we must do something radical if we want to take our lives back and build meaningful, purposeful, and powerful connections with God and others. We must change the way we think.

Romans 12:2 serves as the foundation for this transformation: "Don't copy the behavior and customs of this world, but let God transform you into a new person by changing the way you think. Then you will learn to know God's will for you, which is good and pleasing and perfect." Even if you don't believe that the Bible is true or a valid resource, don't be too quick to dismiss its wisdom. It won't hurt you to take a quick look at something that millions of people have used as a source of guidance and inspiration. And you might learn something.

This verse in Romans simply says that the only way to make progress in life is to stop long enough to reflect on what you're doing. What attitudes and behaviors do you have that only cause you great frustration and disconnect you from God and from other people in your life? What habitual dependencies keep you from taking your life back? Why do you persist in doing them? Where in "the world" did those things come from? Have they been passed down through the generations, did you copy them from someone else, or are they something you made up on your own?

Is it time to abandon them? Of course it is. Are you willing? Only you can answer that question. But we hope the answer is yes because there is no reason to hang onto something that doesn't work and that doesn't move your life forward.

Responsive living begins with a willingness to change the way we think. That is essentially the golden ticket to the Promised Land. It seems so simple and makes so much sense, but we all have a hard time giving up what is comfortable and familiar. *Responsive living begins with a willingness to change the way we think.* Instead, we double down and do more of the same thing—maybe with slight modifications or greater intensity. But doing more of the same will only get you more of the same. When we reflect on what has produced frustration and failure in the past and then commit ourselves to finding new ways, we create hope and potential for a very different future.

So here are some common patterns of thinking to change:

» **Don't think:** *I can change the other person.*

   Start thinking: *I can change* myself, *no matter what the other person does.* It's not your job to motivate change in other people. But that person staring back at you in the mirror? Start there.

» **Don't think:** *Life will get better when the other person gets better.*

   Start thinking: *My life will get better when* I *get better.* When you stop focusing on everything that is wrong with the other people in your life and you begin to focus on the areas in your own life that need improvement or radical change, life will get better.

» **Don't think:** *I'm trapped.*

   Start thinking: *I may feel trapped, but I still have options.* The options you want may not be available today, but if you start working toward making them a reality, you will no longer feel trapped because you will have taken your life back and started to live it in a way that is satisfying and fulfilling.

» **Don't think:** *I've tried everything.*

   Start thinking: *I've tried everything I know how to try, so it's time to connect with someone who can show me some better options.* If you're willing to get help and try some new approaches, your future will have a new sense of hope.

If these examples are not enough to show you how to counter the other-focused, self-defeating thoughts that have prevented you from living freely and fully, my (David's) book *Rethink How You Think* can help you perfect this technique.

Changing our thinking really is transformational in our lives because it takes our focus away from everything in front of us and places it firmly on everything within us.

As scary as that may sound, when we stop focusing on what is so glaringly wrong with other people, it removes a huge burden from our backs. Many people have wasted far too many years living on the other side of the street, in everyone else's lives. But you are meant to live on your *own* side of the street, inhabiting your own life and becoming the person that God intended. You may feel powerless as you begin the long walk back across the street toward home, but you're not helpless. You're not making the journey alone. Help is on the way. Get ready—it's moving day!

"But wait," you say. "I can't go back there quite yet. As I think about going back to my own side of the street, I start to remember why I left in the first place. That's where my real self resides, with all its bad, ugly, abandoned, and confused parts. I don't think I'm ready to face all that. It seems much less painful to stay on the other side of the street for just a little while longer."

What if we were to tell you that it's okay? Moving back to your own side of the street not only means giving up your criticism of other people; it also marks the beginning of a deep friendship with yourself—yes, both the good and the bad. It will involve getting reacquainted with your true self, understanding how you've been hurt, and doing the work of forgiveness that will lead you to wholeness and self-acceptance. You may be surprised to find how compassionate you become with others, as well.

Finding Self-Compassion

As partial or complete dependents, we usually know how to be compassionate toward other people. We care about them, worry about them, help them, and do all kinds of loving things for them. But typically, we are short on compassion for ourselves. We may say some encouraging words to ourselves, but it usually doesn't go very deep or last very long.

What works against us is a sharp inner voice that either drives us compulsively or causes us to give up because everything seems hopeless. The former voice leads to trying harder, while the latter voice says, "Don't bother." Either way, we end up being critical of ourselves, and eventually we may even hate ourselves. Silencing that critical voice is not easy, but it is possible. Here's how to begin—by using your imagination.

First of all, silence that critical inner voice.

Next, think of a situation from when you were growing up. It can be a haunting memory that is very vivid or simply a time when you felt alone and misunderstood. Fill in as many details as possible: What room were you in? What happened? Were you standing, sitting, or lying down? Were you crying, angry, or both? Make the scene as vivid as you can recall.

Once you have a picture of that situation in your mind, enter the scene as an adult and imagine yourself talking with the young *you*. Ask your younger self what he or she is feeling. Provide the comfort you longed for at the time but did not receive. Take your time, even imagining the adult *you* holding the young *you* as you offer comfort and acceptance. If there are tears, let them flow freely. After an amount of time appropriate to the situation, leave the scene and stop the exercise. You may want to journal about the exercise or call a safe person (if you have one) and share what you just experienced.

I (David) have used this exercise with people in my office, and I've found that it actually begins a transforming process that leads to self-acceptance and self-compassion. It changes your perception of your younger self and allows you to stop blaming yourself for the painful things that occurred as you were growing up. It changes the way the adult *you* understands what the young *you* experienced. And it also marks the beginning of a process of acknowledging what you truly experienced as a child.

Self-compassion allows you to stop blaming yourself for the painful things that occurred as you were growing up.

You may want to repeat this exercise using several different scenarios in which the adult *you* offers comfort and compassion to the young *you*. Some people resist this exercise because it feels too much like self-pity or selfishness. But it's important to remember—or to realize—that our woundedness has made us think that any self-care we do is a selfish act. That's how we get stuck in the pain that keeps us on the far side of the street. It's also the voice of the internal critic that wants to keep us stuck.

I often try to get people to differentiate between the terms *selfish* and *self-centered*. *Self-centered* describes the negative connotations we associate with being selfish. There is no positive connotation to self-centeredness. But there is a positive connotation to being selfish— namely, *self-care*. There is no negative sense to the nurturing we give ourselves.

It's time to start developing a plan for the healing process that leads to a responsive life. We'll take it step by step.

Find a safe person with whom to share the healing journey

As much as you may be tempted to try to go it alone, you really cannot venture on this healing journey by yourself. It requires a safe traveling companion to walk alongside you. Solomon reminds us, "Two people are better off than one, for they can help each other succeed. If one person falls, the other can reach out and help. But someone who falls alone is in real trouble."[1]

A safe person is someone you can trust, even if it's difficult for you. Building trust is an important part of the healing process.

A safe person is someone who listens in order to understand and who won't interrupt with a different story unless it helps you both to better understand your story. A safe person is someone who will keep confidential what you share and what you are working on. He or she won't ever share your story as a "prayer request." A safe person is someone you can trust, even if it's difficult for you. Building trust is an important part of the healing process.

Sometimes the only way to find a safe person is to enlist the help of a professional counselor. Counselors have a code of ethics that requires them to be trustworthy. If you choose a professional counselor as your safe person, it will help if he or she understands the Twelve Steps of Life Recovery (see page 167). You have a right to interview a counselor in advance. Once you have found a safe person who will work with you, you are ready for the next step in the healing process.

Several years ago, more than one of my (Steve's) colleagues on the *New Life Live!* radio show suggested that I might benefit from some trauma therapy. When Dr. Sheri Keffer, who has some unique training in this area, came on board at New Life, she emphasized the value of trauma therapy even more. I'm willing to try anything that will help me, so I finally signed up for some work with a trauma specialist. This was after I had been told by Dr. Daniel Amen that a CT scan of my brain indicated I had suffered a traumatic brain injury, most likely from playing football.

As I mentioned in our discussion of the impact of trauma in chapter 8, I made some really big mistakes in the area of relationships and maturity during my senior year of high school. I had lived with the shame of it for decades and had staked out my territory in the land of self-condemnation. It was in one of my sessions with the trauma therapist that I realized I had traumatized myself with self-condemnation long before suffering trauma at the hands of others. Then a new light of connection came on as I realized that these mistakes had occurred after the injuries I sustained playing football. The change in my behavior and decision making after the football season was so dramatically different from my behavior before the season that a head injury was the only explanation that made sense.

During another one of the counseling sessions, my therapist was leading me through a visualizing exercise, and he asked me what I was seeing.

I saw six pallbearers—all six of them identical to me—carrying a casket that was completely transparent. Inside the casket was a totally charred black body that was also mine. In this moving image, I watched as the six Steves dumped the old, burned, dead Steve into a dark swamp, then turned and went back the way they had come. I understood that this symbolized—and made very real for me—my letting go of an old self-image, which was now burned and buried in a swamp. When the session was over, I dried my tears and drove home without a word. But as the day and evening went on, a sense of relief welled up in me, and I experienced peace and rest like never before. And that peace has persisted. I had to be willing to take the first step, but the trauma specialist helped me find a comfortable place of redemption and reconciliation with my past. If you're suffering the effects of trauma, such therapy might do the same for you.

Acknowledge the truth

Healing always begins with an acknowledgment of what happened while we were growing up. I like how *The Living Bible* paraphrases Jeremiah 6:14: "You can't heal a wound by saying it's not there!" The New Living Translation puts it like this: "They offer superficial treatments for my people's mortal wound. They give assurances of peace when there is no peace." We're not doing that here. We are suggesting a healing process that will confront the wounds of our lives head-on.

We are suggesting a healing process that will confront the wounds of our lives head-on.

Later in chapter 6 of Jeremiah, the prophet quotes the Lord as saying, "Stop at the crossroads and look around. Ask for the old, godly way, and walk in it. Travel its path, and you will find rest for your souls."[2] The godly way always begins with a decision to face the truth in love. That's what it means to acknowledge the truth.

We begin by looking at places where we have obviously been wounded. This wounding is often the result of sin—sins we have committed and sins that were committed against us. We are to confess our own sins (see James 5:16 and 1 John 1:9) and forgive those who have sinned against us (see Matthew 6:12). Through forgiveness, God has provided a remedy for both types of sin.

Ask yourself who sinned against you and identify what those sins were. For example, what types of abuse did you experience? Was it neglect? Was it mental, verbal, emotional, sexual, or spiritual abuse, or some combination of them? How severe was the abuse? If you saw another family today do these things to one of their children, would you consider it abuse? Be honest with yourself, because the only person with whom you will share this information at this point (maybe ever) is the safe person you chose. Be careful not to minimize what you experienced. We want to pull up this weed by the roots.

Next, look at your attachment issues, beginning with any you have in your adult relationships. Are you typically a loner? Do you feel self-sufficient? Are you anxious and clingy in your relationships? Are you fearful about how others see you? Do you tend to run either hot or cold in how you relate to others? Are the issues clear in your mind or fuzzy?

What about the traumas you've experienced over the years? Again, don't minimize what has happened to you. Have you experienced any betrayals, either while growing up or as an adult? Has anyone you were close to ever died suddenly? What about being abandoned by a parent, either through death or divorce? That would have a traumatic effect on anyone. Have you experienced anything else that would be considered a trauma? Talk about these things with your safe person. Then move on to the next phase.

Identify your basic emotional posture

There are many ways to evaluate our emotional character, but for our purposes here, the most effective method is to identify four consistent emotional responses that typify our approach to life. Most theorists identify six basic emotions—joy, surprise, fear, anger, sadness, and shame—and our approach is based on the four negative ones: fear, anger, shame, and sadness. Some practitioners refer to disgust instead of shame, but when dealing with issues of codependency, shame is a more relevant term to use.

What is your basic emotional posture when faced with high stress or an emotional crisis? Almost every codependent behavior pattern begins from a posture of fear. We're afraid of what others might think of us. Will they like us? Will they accept us? Will they be nice to us? Questions like these are rooted in a posture of fear. Part of our healing is to learn how to face what we fear and conquer it.

People who are too focused on other people's problems may approach their relationships from a position of anger. They often express their anger in passive ways that are hard to identify, but their baseline posture is clearly anger. They entertain thoughts such as *Why is it always up to me?* or *Why can't they handle this better? It is so tiring to always have to take care of this for them.* When asked to do something they may say no, but eventually they comply. An angry posture may quickly become an attitude of resentment, in which we reluctantly perform codependent behaviors out of obligation, but without bothering to mask our resentment with caring. Anger is often the position taken by people who still need to face up to and process some deep hurts.

Anger is often the position taken by people who still need to face up to and process some deep hurts.

Shame can be a confusing emotional posture. There is a healthy shame that we feel when we've done something wrong. Its purpose is to motivate us to make things right. Healthy shame is a component of a healthy conscience, which motivates us to self-correct. But there is also a toxic shame that is unrelated to anything we've done but is rooted in how we view ourselves. And how we view ourselves is very often a reflection of how we were treated while growing up.

Toxic shame goes beyond self-criticism, which is a natural part of who we are. Self-criticism focuses on our *behavior* (what we've done), whereas toxic shame focuses on our *self-image*—what a bad, flawed, ugly person we really are. Shame-based codependency is an attempt to cover up our feelings of worthlessness by pretending we care about other people.

Talk things over with your safe person to identify your basic emotional posture. Once you've identified your basic emotional foundation, you will be able to explore and confront the reasons why you operate from that particular posture, and you will begin to determine whether to confront and challenge the fear, anger, or shame. (Sadness as an emotional posture is typically reserved for the grieving stage of recovery, which we will discuss later in the chapter.)

Name what happened to you

One of the most powerful actions you can take is to give a name to what happened to you. It is about speaking the truth. To name something is to take authority over it. It is an empowering action. It's something we have done since we were little. We named our dolls, our teddy bears, and our pets. There is intrinsic satisfaction in that ability.

In some pagan cultures in the ancient Near East, a person's real name was a secret, known only to a trusted few. In these cultures, they believed that if someone knew your real name, he or she had power over you. We see Jesus exercise the power of naming when he gives

> *One of the most powerful actions you can take is to give a name to what happened to you. It is about speaking the truth. To name something is to take authority over it.*

Simon the name Peter. Saul's name was changed to Paul after his conversion. This renaming marked a new identity in both men's lives. The power of a name is also seen in Peter's declaration to the lame man outside the Temple: "I don't have any silver or gold for you. But I'll give you what I have. In the name of Jesus Christ the Nazarene, get up and walk!"[3] There is healing power in the name of Jesus.

Exercise that power now by naming what happened to you. For example, you might say, "I'm a recovering codependent who was emotionally and verbally abused as a child. I'm going to name that period in my life 'my time in exile,' and I am now in 'the land of healing.'" You can name what happened to you as a child, or any chronic distress you've experienced, or you can give a name to the belief systems you held as part of your false self.

The name you choose should not be aimed at another person. The point is not to express our anger or tear someone down verbally. The naming should be about yourself. I (David) refer to the season when one of my kids got caught up in the drug culture as "my days of ignorance." My recovery involved becoming educated, doing things that didn't make logical sense, and trusting some people who knew how to work with addictions. But that's still my name for that period of time.

Once you have truthfully named the important parts of what you experienced, it's time to move on to the next step, which involves processing your grief.

Grieve what was lost

As you acknowledge the truth about what has happened to you, it becomes clear that something was lost during that time and that it's still lost today. Based on what we've learned about our woundedness, abandonment issues, fears, anger, and shame, we can say that the primary loss has been the loss of our real self. We lost our sense of who we are because we felt unaccepted, unappreciated, and uninformed, and we were isolated from genuine love and comfort.

Grieving emotional losses is a four-stage process that cannot be rushed through. Because we have lived for so long through our false selves and considered it normal, we must begin by refamiliarizing ourselves with what we have lost, moving from unawareness to awareness. Because we had to bury our true self in order to live through a false self, we must undertake an excavation process by which we re-identify—and re-identify with—what we've lost. That's the process we began when we named what has happened to us.

By identifying the losses we are going to grieve, we begin to grapple with two interwoven facets of grief: anger and sadness.

By identifying the losses we are going to grieve, we begin to grapple with two interwoven facets of grief: anger and sadness. Anger is a form of protest: "That's not the way it was supposed to be!" We know what we missed, and we're not happy about it. It was wrong! The flip side to protest is the sadness and resignation that we feel.

Men tend to embrace the anger and protest part of grieving, but they may get stuck on the sadness part. Weeping over what was lost can seem like crying over spilt milk. It doesn't feel manly.

Women tend to embrace the sadness, but they have a more difficult time with the anger and protest. Many women, when they tap into their anger, quickly return to the tears and the sadness.

Therapeutic grieving requires both anger (protest) and sadness (resignation). If you are having difficulty with one or the other, try writing either an angry letter or a sad letter to those who withheld from you what was lost. This letter is for your eyes only. It's okay to share it with your safe person, but *never* send it to anyone else. It is simply a tool to help you grieve.

Eventually, grieving must lead to forgiveness. After all, that's what God did with *our* failures. He forgave all our sins. With that great, undeserved forgiveness in view, there is really nothing that can happen in our lives or in our families that is beyond forgiveness. How long the forgiving process will take, however, will depend on how early in your life you were wounded and how deep the wounds go.

Eventually, grieving must lead to forgiveness. After all, that's what God did with our failures. He forgave all our sins.

Some have likened this part of the healing process to peeling an onion. We have to work our way toward the core—and it may not happen without tears! Grieving is not something we do once and for all. It may need to be repeated as we become aware of deeper issues. But the desired outcome and resolution is always forgiveness.

Now that you've come this far, congratulations on your commitment to becoming healed. Now we will look at the important issue of defining healthy perimeters and how to say no so that our *yes* has meaning.

12

BECOMING A DECIDER, A DEFENDER, AND A DEVELOPER

As you begin to take your life back—from the control of another person, an addiction to a substance or habit, or the residue of a shame-filled past—you may soon come to realize that three very important qualities are either underdeveloped in your character or missing altogether. These are the abilities to *decide, defend,* and *develop.* You may have conceded them to someone else out of weakness or confusion, or as part of a defective survival strategy. Or they may have been taken from you—stolen outright by someone who discounted or ignored the value of your identity as a person uniquely created in the image of God.

Without these vital building blocks, you will continue to stumble along as you try to get by on your own. Fortunately, you are no longer consigned to existing in a constant state of *reaction.* You now have the freedom to overcome the familiar obstacles of passivity, compliance, and blind service and to *respond* to God's call with everything you have.

No longer will you live in the shadow of shame. No longer will you allow your life to be overcome with unresolved emotional turmoil, untreated dependency, or uninvited intrusions of any kind or from any source. If there's a battle cry welling up from the depths of your soul, it will surely be "Victim No More!" (It feels good just to write those words!)

But before we examine how to become a decider, defender, and developer, a word of caution is in order, lest you sabotage the potential for better that is just within your reach.

As you learn how to draw some healthy new lines of demarcation, we don't want you to overrespond by erecting walls topped with barbed wire when a white picket fence would do just fine. The purpose of deciding, defending, and developing is to create room for yourself in your relationships, not to put up barriers to keep other people out. We want you to be able to define your territory without laying a minefield where other people will never be welcome, never be allowed to ask forgiveness, or never receive permission to make restitution.

Wouldn't it be sad if—after years of being ignored, minimized, abused, or alienated—you put up walls that made you more isolated than ever? Ultimately, we all want the best that God has for us, even if it means temporary discomfort in the short term. We want flexible borders, not impenetrable walls. When our motive is to honor God, the pain that comes from doing the right thing will be redemptive pain that leads to something better.

When our motive is to honor God, the pain that comes from doing the right thing will be redemptive pain that leads to something better.

Austin and Kathy dated for two or three years before they got married. Both had a strong faith, and they were always talking about doing the right thing when it came to their relationship. The wedding day finally arrived, but hidden storm clouds came with it. Within a week, it was clear that the honeymoon was over. Unrealized and unmet expectations during the first few days of marriage put their relationship on rocky ground before they even got their feet under them.

Now that Austin had "secured the prize," his attention turned to other priorities in his life. Although he had always put his best foot forward in courting Kathy, he quickly reverted to business as usual in his daily routine. And though he would never state it in such crass terms, there was a part of him that was relieved to no longer feel the pressure to constantly woo her. In fact, things about her that had never bothered him before now became instant irritations, and he let her know it. There was such a radical disconnect between pre-wedding Austin and his postwedding persona that Kathy was shocked and deeply hurt.

She immediately went to a counselor and told Austin that he had better get one for himself if he didn't want to be telling his friends that he had blown up his marriage in less than ten days. Though disillusioned, she said she would stay in the marriage if he would get help.

When Austin went in for counseling, the therapist was able to show him how all the barriers to vulnerability he had lowered in order to attract Kathy had been raised up again once the vows were said. The counselor explained how fear had played a strong role in Austin's defensiveness when Kathy tried to reconnect with him after he had settled back into the world inside his head—a world she didn't know existed. The counselor was also able to connect the dots for Austin, showing him how his mother had drawn him in and then abandoned him when he was younger. After a couple of sessions, he was ready to do whatever it took to win Kathy back.

Unfortunately, Kathy's counselor took a different approach.

Everything she said affirmed Kathy and strengthened her, but it led Kathy to build walls that became obstacles in the marriage relationship. She counseled Kathy to refuse to sleep in the same room with Austin, or even interact with him, for thirty days. The therapist called it a cooling-off period, but it really stoked a fire of resentment and misunderstanding instead. It was a radical reaction to the hurt that Austin had caused.

During the time when Austin was taking a look at himself and was willing to acknowledge how he had created a nightmare of a marriage for both of them, Kathy would not even allow him to tell her what he was learning and coming to understand. Ultimately, she constructed an impenetrable wall that she never took down, and within a year they were divorced.

Walls of protection can definitely keep us from getting hurt, but they will also damage a relationship if they offer no way for the other person to break through.

Walls of protection can definitely keep us from getting hurt, but they will also damage a relationship if they offer no way for the other person to break through. It helps to be aware of the walls we've built, and to be willing to destroy those walls and replace them with firm but flexible borders that allow others to get through and connect with us heart to heart.

If you feel uneasy or even a bit panicky as you are reading this, wondering whether you have misunderstood, misappropriated, or misapplied what you thought were healthy, God-honoring principles for establishing boundaries, we encourage you to continue reading. When you start to take your life back, you might be afraid that you'll go overboard and wall off God's work in your life or in the lives of your loved ones. But if your spirit remains willing, the Holy Spirit will help you see the areas where you have taken a healthy concept to an unhealthy extreme. To set your mind at ease, it might help if we clarify some things about unhealthy walls.

First of all, we must remember that we all are flawed human beings. We all build aspects of our lives that are defective. Fortunately, character construction that is not up to code can be reworked in line with God's standards. This awareness could lead to the breakthrough you've been looking for that will allow God to work in your life in ways you haven't seen before. Jesus, the Master Carpenter, is used to seeing defective work and turning it into something magnificent. This could be the beginning of a transformation of healing and wholeness in your life.

The only thing worse than building a wall is not building anything at all. Defective walls can be torn down, but complete inaction or resistance is impossible to counter. Denial, resistance, and passive inaction are prisons that we hope we have left behind. Here are some construction guidelines that we hope will help you.

Learning to Decide

A life that has been taken back is a safe and secure place to live. We are not tossed to and fro by the whims and whams of other people. We remain free to be ourselves, free to choose, free to heal, and free to be mature adults. As we begin to see transformation in our souls, we realize that we don't have to *react* to every little thing that might threaten our comfort or safety. Instead, we are able to *respond* in a mature way and *choose* the best decision. With healthy demarcations, we know where other people end and we begin. We know that our loved ones are entitled to communicate with us, engage with us, and love us in healthy and appropriate ways, and we decide to allow that to happen, even facilitating the process. We allow other people room for their defects and imperfections, and we decide not to allow those defects and imperfections to hurt us or dominate us—or even to affect our thoughts and feelings. When we hold the title to our own lives and maintain full ownership of who God made us to be, we decide to experience connection, healthy attachment, and attunement to other people. And we make bold decisions not to allow evil to be done to us or to others.

As we rediscover our real self and begin to live comfortably without pretense or façades, we develop standards that we intend to keep and that we expect others to honor.

As we rediscover our real self and begin to live comfortably without pretense or facades, we develop standards that we intend to keep and that we expect others to honor. They provide a measure of certainty, consistency, and reliability in our relationships.

One example that may help us understand healthy standards is the subject of sex in a marriage relationship. The Bible clearly teaches that spouses are not to withhold sex from each other.[1] That is a profound truth that is easy to understand. It's also easy to see what can happen if we don't abide by it. If we withhold sex within marriage, we prevent or undermine a deeper connection, fail to keep the commitment we made when we married, and open up ourselves and our spouses to temptation and vulnerability. A healthy sexual standard allows for mutual agreement about timing and frequency—and even allows for times of abstinence—but the underlying agreement is to pursue intimacy. Because sex within a marriage binds the couple together and builds their relationship, it is a biblical mandate that makes very good sense.

Let us say one more thing about this example for anyone who may be saying, "Yes, but . . ."

Healthy sexual standards and practices in a marriage mean that sex will never become coercive or manipulative. If that has happened in your marriage, it is a violation of your real self and an act of defiance against the God who created you. Likewise, both spouses should reasonably be able to expect protection from insults or abuse. Soul protection is as important—and even more justifiable—than protection of the body. Emotional abuse and insults eat at the very core of the soul.

If a wife tells her husband that he is worthless and a loser because he lost his job, and if she reinforces that message until he finds new employment, he has an obligation to protect himself from those harmful words. If a husband tells his wife that she is not what he thought she would be, not what he wants, or not what he deserves, she has an obligation to protect herself from those abusive statements.

The behavioral standard and expected response in both cases is the same: "I have made a healthy decision not to remain in the presence of that kind of treatment."

Learning to Defend

When we live with healthy standards and limits, we don't allow others to become our "deciders." We also learn that it is a sign of growth when we decide to become our own strongest defender.

We're not talking about becoming defensive whenever someone points out a defect or flaw that needs our attention. We're talking about deciding that we have rights and responsibilities that must be defended. We decide that we will no longer be used by others as if we have no worth or will. When appropriate, we will defend our right to be who God has created us to be, and we will defend ourselves with the most powerful two-letter word in the English language: no.

Saying no as a positive response that preserves our freedom might come in several forms:

» Asking an abuser to stop
» Demanding that abuse stop
» Leaving the room
» Leaving the house
» Asking the other person to leave the room
» Asking the other person to leave the house
» Asking the other person to make a call in order to get help immediately

» Making the call yourself to get help
» Scheduling a counseling meeting and asking the other person to show up
» Getting help from a wise counselor, plotting a path to resolve the problem, and following through to create an opportunity for the best possible outcome

All of the above options are healthy alternatives when you decide you are worth defending and when you step up to do so. They protect the involved parties and foster freedom. They are respectful of goodness and things that are right. They are the opposite of enabling evil, waiting for God to do what we should be doing, or passively wishing that things would get better on their own. They are clear reflections of a heart that is open to repair and restoration while defending against control and manipulation.

Defending is the opposite of building a life-killing, hope-destroying wall. Walls keep people locked into the past with no hope for a different future.

Defending is the opposite of building a life-killing, hope-destroying wall. Walls keep people locked into the past with no hope for a different future. Walls cut off options and connections. Walls create obstacles that we bump up against every day. Relational walls are built with bricks of shame, regret, and despair. The mortar that holds the bricks together is deep, unrelenting resentment—Satan's superglue, which he uses to wall us off from everything sacred. Sadly, we might willingly help with the construction of these evil walls. We then sit behind them and seethe and resent, demand and control, all the while wondering why we went to so much trouble to take our lives back.

Occasionally, we look outside our walls to see if anything has changed. When it hasn't, we hunker back down, dig in our heels, and vow to ourselves to hold the fort. Meanwhile, we are missing God's best for our lives and essentially bouncing from one extreme of defective living to the other. Both David and I have done this, and fortunately we've both seen the error of our ways. Every healthy relationship needs two healthy deciders and defenders working together in full ownership of their lives, with no need for deadly walls.

Knowing When to Say No

Tough and appropriate love requires a decision to say no to things that deserve a no, but we should not say no just because we can. I (Steve) worked with a man who had been very unhappy in his previous job because his wisdom and experience were often ignored. It seemed that every project to which he would have said no was funded anyway. If his advice had been followed, many bad and costly decisions could have been avoided, but his discernment and expertise were overlooked and undervalued in the decision-making process.

On his first day of work in our organization, I met with him and told him he would have the ability to say no in his new job. We would honor his judgment and allow him to veto things that he believed should not be funded. But I told him that he also had to evaluate every no to make sure he wasn't saying it just because he could or as a reaction to his previous situation. He—and we—needed to be certain that he was not going to become a negative influence in our organization just because he had not been honored in his previous job. It was insurance against reactive living and encouragement for him to be responsibly responsive.

Some people inappropriately disapprove of everything because it feels safer to say no. It feels more protective, but it can be as big an obstacle, or wall, as any other defective coping device. Two obvious examples are the anorexic who says no to the food that would be nourishing and life-giving, or the agoraphobic who says no to leaving the house. In such cases, the *no* is clearly pathological.

When an avoider says no to engagement and interaction, it kills the relationship. An inappropriate no can be just as dangerous as a risky yes that gets us into unhealthy, life-stealing situations and relationships. So we need some good guidelines for when to say no. Here are a few:

» Before we say no, we must be certain we are denying or rejecting what is wrong and defective and not saying no for some other reason, such as fear, withholding, acting in, or revenge.
» We must say no when saying yes would enable or encourage evil.
» *No* is always the right answer when our health or welfare is needlessly jeopardized by a controlling or manipulative person.
» We must not say no when we are called upon to be courageous. We must do what needs to be done, when it needs to be done, no matter the consequences.
» We should say no when the reason for saying yes would only be to avoid conflict or avoid exerting energy.
» We should say no to something good when we can say yes to something better.
» We should say no when we are tempted to repeat the same old failed strategies that never have helped us take our lives back, and never will.
» *No* is never the right answer when it is punitive, vengeful, mean, or manipulative of another person.
» *No* is never the right answer when *yes* would open the door of opportunity for healing and wholeness.
» *No* is never the right answer just because it feels safe. God would have us risk a little more to experience his fullness in our lives.

If *yes* is just too scary, find out why you feel that way and work through it, discovering the source of the fear or the need to use fear to control or dominate someone else. If *no* is your default answer even when God offers wonderful opportunities, find out why and commit to resolving it. The response of a simple *no* restricts and restrains, but it isn't always the best answer. When we take our lives back, we become free to say no when *no* is best; but we're also free to say yes without fear.

Deciders and Defenders Use Tough Love

Some would say that all love is tough. I (Steve) told a group just the other day that a marriage license is really just a work permit. Marriage is work, and it can be tough; but when someone else owns your life, deciding to use tough love to defend your real self is what will allow you to take your life back. Tough love says that I will choose to not give you what you *want* if it prevents you from attaining what you *need* or if it would prevent me from becoming the person I want and need to be. Tough love requires a courage that most people-pleasers don't have, so they must bring others into their camp for support, guidance, and accountability in order to defend their right to own their own lives. The courage of a defense team battling for your soul can compensate for your individual lack of courage. God says he will never allow us to be tempted beyond what we can bear, but that doesn't mean we'll be able to bear every temptation *alone*.[2] Sometimes we need the help of others to find God's promised way of escape or to bear up under our burdens and endure.[3]

Learning How to Become a Developer

If all we ever do is decide not to allow someone to hurt or control us, we will be safe, but we will find ourselves stuck forever right where we are. Likewise, if all we do is defend what is good and wonderfully made within us, we will be affirmed, but we won't get very far beyond where we are right now. Obviously, we need to do more than decide to say no and defend our independence. That is why we need to become developers.

Developers continually ask a simple question: "Now what do we need to do?" Perhaps we need to practice a little bit of tough love on *ourselves* rather than on someone else. Wallowing in the past and obsessing over what was and what might have been can become a comfortable place of inaction. Self-shaming over missed opportunities and blown chances is not a recipe for healthy, responsive living. Tough self-love puts a stop to that by establishing a limit and putting up a healthy border between our current lives and the past. From our side of the street or our side of the fence, we can glance through the pickets at the past but not allow the past to control us or own us. We can evaluate and learn from what led us to make some devastating choices, but we don't have to relive or rehash the consequences of those choices.

Developers continually ask a simple question: "Now what do we need to do?" Perhaps we need to practice a little bit of tough love on ourselves *rather than on someone else.*

We can look at the sources of our shame without cloaking ourselves in the darkness of that shame. Tough self-love helps us to be honest about things that are uncomfortable instead of becoming people-pleasers and hiding from the truth. If we receive nourishing and restorative care from others, we can be tough enough to stop ourselves from languishing in memories and regrets from the past that rob us of our present joy and cloud the future. Sometimes, tough self-love is the best kind of love of all.

Everybody Needs a Developer Who Knows When and How to Say Yes

When we fully understand the concept of establishing healthy, protective, and firm but flexible borders, we realize that sometimes we don't need them—not even good and healthy ones. We never need a wall that will close us off from our loved ones. What we need is the freedom to say yes to things that are life-giving and life-affirming without clouding the issue by defining limitations. There are times when the way forward is a *yes*, but to get to *yes*, we must give up some ground that may have become sacred to us. Or we may have to give up some justifiable resentments or enshrined entitlements. When we do, we may take our lives back and take our loved ones along with us. As with anything in life, we need the right tool for the right job. There is no one-size-fits-all solution for every challenge we encounter.

Recently, I (Steve) had a conversation with a woman at an Ultimate Intimacy Intensive Workshop put on by New Life. Brooke told me she had been married to an uncaring man who would not give her what she wanted and needed. In response to his detachment, she might have put up a wall that would have removed any possibility of connection until he finally delivered on what she wanted. But she hadn't done that. The lines of communication were still open. She also might have made *no* her default answer until her husband, Gary, at least came up to a minimum standard of attentiveness or looked as if he was putting forth some effort. But she had avoided that pitfall as well.

By the way, she and I were having this conversation with Gary sitting right next to me and across the table from her. He and I had been discussing widescreen televisions, and I was quite envious of his seventy-five-inch HD plasma. Here I was getting by with a mere sixty-five-inch screen. Go figure. But when Gary told me that they would be turning off that television more often after this weekend workshop, his wife looked at him adoringly and said, "He's my seventy-five-inch widescreen television."

Brooke went on to say that before coming to the workshop, she had been full of bitterness and resentment and had been ready to give up completely on their marriage. She had told Gary what she needed and had explained what she wanted from him, and he had never delivered—not once. In her mind, he was the most uncaring and unresponsive spouse she could have ever gotten stuck with. She could not understand how a man who said he loved her—over and over again—could fall so short of the mark. Not only that, but he would also get upset with her when she became upset with him.

You might think this kind of dynamic would have caused Brooke to build a protective wall so she wouldn't be hurt or disappointed again. But that hadn't happened. In fact, she and Gary were at the workshop precisely because there were no unscalable walls between them. They were willing to listen to whatever God might say to them through the speakers, therapists, and other attendees. And what they heard changed everything.

Brooke finally realized that, in all the time they'd been married, Gary had had no idea what she was talking about when she told him what she wanted or needed. It was as if they spoke two separate languages and were trying to communicate in a third language. There was simply no way for him to understand the concepts of *attunement, attachment, emotional bonding,* and *intimacy* because those things had never been taught or modeled in the home he grew up in. He had been taught that men were designed to be strong and independent and that he should courageously hide his feelings if he ever felt the need to share them. Tough, not tender. In control and in charge, not vulnerable. Providing faithfully for his family, with no need to do anything except lead.

As a result of the weekend workshop, Brooke became aware that her expectations of Gary were the emotional equivalent of marrying a man with two broken legs and his arm in a sling and expecting him to carry her across the threshold, run a marathon, and walk an extra mile whenever possible. The truth was, Gary was emotionally challenged and lacked the training and experience to do what she expected.

Both Brooke and Gary understood their situation for the first time. He understood that he didn't know the language of emotion— but he wanted to learn it. Brooke said that when Gary began to learn some emotional vocabulary during one of the workshop exercises and they caught a glimpse of how things could be, she fell madly in love with him all over again.

Taking your life back is not just about deciding to defend yourself. It is about finding and removing roadblocks that have disconnected you from other people.

Taking your life back is not just about deciding to defend yourself. It is about finding and removing roadblocks, sinkholes, and dead ends that have disconnected you from other people and stopped your journey from going forward together. Sometimes we don't need another decision to defend; we need an invitation to press in and allow the developer within us to do the job of developing every positive characteristic that God intends us to have. Sometimes we need a new understanding, or we need to transform our relationships and our lives by changing how we think about ourselves and how we think about the people who are falling short of our expectations. But we never need a wall.

We all are familiar with glass-half-full and glass-half-empty people. But there's another dichotomy—between *why?* people and *why not?* people—that can help us understand when to decide between our defending and our developing. If every question or opportunity in life is met with a "Why?" or a "Why should I?" we are constantly being shut down and silenced by a default *no* decision from a defective inner defender.

Why not? people are willing to look at the possibilities that lie ahead and decide to allow the developer to go to work. There may be very good reasons not to do something, but healthy deciders are open to changes and opportunities that their inner developers are ready to implement. They are aware that *no* is sometimes—maybe even often—the correct response in choosing to do the right thing; but they remain open to God's guidance, and they allow their inner decider, defender, and developer to be controlled by the divine Director. They say yes after considering the benefits of a decision, even if it is scary to go in the direction of yes. But they also weigh the costs and the risks so that they don't inappropriately say yes to everything. In saying, "Why not?" their aim is to take back dimensions of their lives that may have been dominated by fear, insecurity, overly protective vows, or irrational generalizations about people or the past. As with any way of life, saying yes is best done in consultation with wise counselors, sponsors, friends, and family members who love us and who know that our ultimate motivation is to live out God's plan and purposes for our lives.

Taking Back a Dating Life for Marrieds

One way to say yes in a marriage is to take back your dating life, especially if it has been shut down completely by busyness, conflict, or fatigue. We know that couples who reserve time for themselves— essentially saying yes to the relationship over everything else—find more satisfaction than those who don't make time. When we stop trying to find the next excuse to distance ourselves, to disconnect, or to build a wall, we can start to say yes to dating and having fun, just as when we were single way back when. If you take back your dating life, you might be taking back your marriage. Saying yes to one key aspect of your relationship may turn out to be the yes that the entire relationship needs. *Yes* creates a wide-open gate that draws people out from behind their protective walls and back into constructive engagement.

Taking Back a Dating Life for Singles

If ever there were someone who needed a strong system of deciding and defending, it would be a single person who is dating. There are so many unhealthy, ungodly forms of dating that most people would benefit from having some guidelines. On the other hand, we don't want to become so overly cautious and fear based that we close down potentially valuable relationships before they have a chance to form. If your beliefs about dating have become overly negative, you may need to cautiously but purposefully take back your dating life and see what God might have in store for you.

Yes creates a wide open gate that draws people out from behind their protective walls and back into constructive engagement.

If you are not in possession of your dating life, maybe it is because you say no to every possibility. If you are fearful, find ways to create safety—such as meeting in a safe, low-key environment or starting with a group date accompanied by trusted friends. Counseling, creativity, double- or triple-dating, group activities, learning new hobbies, or volunteering at places where compatible people may be found are all ways to take back your dating life along with the rest of your life.

A Paradoxical Ending

The end of one thing is often the beginning of something else. When it comes to establishing the healthy practices of deciding, defending, and developing, you can stop the detrimental wall-building in order to pursue healthier options. But you will never establish healthy internal resources if you don't stop long enough to evaluate both what you have done in the past and the position you're currently in. Here are some guidelines for establishing the three key components of deciding, defending, and developing that will help you take your life back.

» Ask yourself who, if anyone, is controlling you or attempting to control you.

» Identify destructive or unhelpful habits, behaviors, patterns, or addictions that control too much of your life.

» Consider the possibility that your problem has a physical cause or contributor. For example, you may have a chemical or hormonal imbalance, or the emotional centers in your brain may have a functional defect. Talk to your doctor to get a diagnosis.

» Become aware of your reactions to the controlling forces that are robbing you of the life that God intended for you. We cannot always change our circumstances, but we can change how we respond to our circumstances.

» Evaluate where you need to establish boundaries or where you have allowed a boundary to lapse.

» Evaluate boundaries you have established in places where they don't need to be. How have they prevented you from moving forward rather than protecting you from getting stuck?

» Assess your relationships to identify where you have built unscalable walls. Why have these walls been built and maintained? How may they be replaced by healthy boundaries?

» Identify people, places, and situations that have prompted you to say no as an overreaction based on fear, rage, or shame.

» Work with a sponsor or a trusted therapist to uncover the sources of your overreactions and work to resolve those sources of pain, fear, or intense anger.

» Consult a trusted therapist who can help you identify areas where you can say yes to a new life, and who can show you how to safely implement a yes-filled life.

Too often, we live someone else's life because we allow ourselves to be controlled by other people, fear, or shame. We must decide to do whatever is necessary to take our lives back and live for God with purpose and meaning. It may not be easy, but we have an obligation to be good defenders and developers of the gifts that God has given us—including the gift of life. Decide right now that when you wake up in the morning, you will do whatever it takes to develop the gift of your life in honor of the one who gave it to you. When you become the decider, defender, and developer of your life, you will tear down any walls that are unhealthy, and you will take important steps toward taking your life back and giving it to God.

13

EXPANDING YOUR
RECOVERY PLAN

As YOU BEGIN to assemble a responsive plan for taking your life back—renewing your mind by changing the way you think; finding self-compassion and a safe person to share your healing journey; acknowledging the truth about your past; identifying your basic emotional posture; naming what happened to you; grieving what was lost; tearing down walls and establishing healthy boundaries—you will reach a point where you will begin to see that an effective way to expand your recovery is by working the Twelve Steps of Life Recovery with your safe person.

Why the Twelve Steps? For several reasons. First, the Twelve Steps were developed from the Bible. The founders of the Twelve Step process, along with their wives, were strong believers in God. In the early stages of developing the Twelve Steps, many of the meetings were simply Bible studies.

In church settings, many of us expend a lot of effort to present ourselves in a positive light. That means we don't share much of who we are, and we are very reluctant to share any of our struggles. We want to look good, plain and simple. And that squeezes to the margins our desire to know other people honestly and to be known. As a result, our problems continue to grow. But that's not the way healing and recovery works, and it's not the way the church is intended to function.

It was different in the early church. Those first generations of Christians were connected to, and open with, one another.

> All the believers met together in one place and shared everything they had. They sold their property and possessions and shared the money with those in need. They worshiped together at the Temple each day, met in homes for the Lord's Supper, and shared their meals with great joy and generosity.[1]

These people not only were generous with each other and shared their joys, but also shared their problems—putting into practice James's injunction to "confess your sins to each other and pray for each other so that you may be healed."[2] When they practiced confession and prayer with each other, their problems grew smaller, and they experienced physical, emotional, and relational healing.

We need to be open to one another, connected, confessing, and sharing our struggles as well as our joys within our relationships.

From these two biblical examples, we again affirm that Life Recovery cannot be accomplished in isolation. When we think we can do it alone, nothing changes. That's just a fact of life. We need to be open to one another, connected, confessing, and sharing our struggles as well as our joys within our relationships. So the key, as it was with the grieving process, is to expand our recovery by working the Twelve Steps with a safe person or safe people—ones with whom we can honestly be ourselves. Let's look at how working the Twelve Steps of Life Recovery expands our healing.

The Twelve Steps of Life Recovery

1. We admitted we were powerless over our problems and that our lives had become unmanageable.
2. We came to believe that a Power greater than ourselves could restore us to sanity.
3. We made a decision to turn our wills and our lives over to the care of God.
4. We made a searching and fearless moral inventory of ourselves.
5. We admitted to God, to ourselves, and to another human being the exact nature of our wrongs.
6. We were entirely ready to have God remove all these defects of character.
7. We humbly asked God to remove our shortcomings.
8. We made a list of all persons we had harmed and became willing to make amends to them all.
9. We made direct amends to such people wherever possible, except when to do so would injure them or others.
10. We continued to take personal inventory, and when we were wrong, promptly admitted it.
11. We sought through prayer and meditation to improve our conscious contact with God, praying only for knowledge of his will for us and the power to carry it out.
12. Having had a spiritual awakening as the result of these Steps, we tried to carry this message to others, and to practice these principles in all our affairs.

(The Twelve Steps of Life Recovery have been adapted with permission from the Twelve Steps of Alcoholics Anonymous.)

Steps 1–3: Our Relationship with Jesus, Our Higher Power

The Twelve Steps of Life Recovery is a comprehensive program that covers our relationships with God, with ourselves, and with others. It doesn't leave anyone out. In order to take your life back, you have to work on all three relationships—and the order is important. Dr. Bob, who was one of the early pioneers of Twelve Step recovery programs, asked newcomers two important questions:

> » Do you believe in God?
> » Have you given your life to Jesus Christ as Lord and Savior?

If the people couldn't answer both questions in the affirmative, Dr. Bob believed they were not ready to begin recovery.

The first three Steps are about our relationship with God, beginning with the recognition that our lives are out of control and that all our attempts to control things haven't changed anything. We need help from a force or power that is greater than ourselves and outside of ourselves. And then we must be willing to turn our wills and lives over to that power.

The Steps are phrased in such a way that they take us beyond mere mental assent. We have to actually give our lives over to God. Some of us have tried that for years. We keep trying to give our lives to God and ask him for help, and it hasn't changed anything. That's because something was left out.

Step 3 says, "We made a *decision* to turn our *wills* and our lives over to the care of God."[3] Relating to God, the "Power greater than ourselves" from Step 2, involves a decision that not only includes our *lives*, but also our *wills*. That means we have *surrendered*. We no longer seek our *own* will—what *we* want; instead, we seek to know and do *God's will* for our lives.

Jesus says, "Anyone who chooses to do the will of God will find out whether my teaching comes from God or whether I speak on my own."[4] If we *choose* to be *willing* to *believe*, we will discover in the *doing* what God's will is. Our willingness to believe leads to belief and then to deeper and more certain belief. It's like digging down to set an anchor in bedrock. You must choose to turn that first shovelful.

The struggle that some people have with surrendering their will and lives to Jesus as their higher power may derive from a common portrayal of Jesus as gentle, meek, and mild. We want someone who is powerful, forceful, and assertive, don't we?

The characteristics of gentleness, meekness, and mildness as commonly understood today do not present an accurate picture of the Jesus revealed in the Bible.

But the characteristics of gentleness, meekness, and mildness as commonly understood today do not present an accurate picture of the Jesus revealed in the Bible. For starters, gentleness and meekness, far from equating to weakness, are perhaps better understood as "great power under control." Given the immense authority that Jesus wielded in human form, was there any other way he could have presented himself to the world that would not have completely overwhelmed everyone? Take a look at what happened in the garden of Gethsemane, when Jesus announced himself to those who had come to arrest him: "As Jesus said 'I Am he,' they all drew back and fell to the ground!"[5] These were soldiers and guardsmen with "blazing torches, lanterns, and weapons,"[6] falling like tenpins.

Likewise, Jesus' mildness suggests the emotional quality of someone who knows exactly who he is and yet doesn't feel the need to impose himself on anyone. Again, he displays power under control, like a thoroughbred responding to the pull of the reins.

Or consider the time when Jesus and the disciples took a boat across the Sea of Galilee and a great storm came up. Several of the disciples were fishermen, who would have spent many hours on that same lake and would have seen many storms. But this one was different, and they were afraid for their lives. Meanwhile, Jesus was asleep in the back of the boat.

The panicked disciples awakened Jesus, saying, "Lord, save us! We're going to drown!" Jesus first rebuked them for their lack of faith, then "got up and rebuked the wind and waves."

"Suddenly there was a great calm."[7] What's not to like about that "higher power"?

One more example is found in Matthew 14:22-34. Again the disciples were in a boat crossing the lake, and again the winds came up and the sea was rough. But this time, Jesus wasn't even with them—until they got about halfway across the lake, at which point he appeared, walking toward them on the water. The disciples were terrified, thinking he was a ghost. But Jesus said, "Take courage. I am here!"

Now, imagine that you were Peter and you said to Jesus, "Lord, if it's really you, tell me to come to you, walking on the water." Jesus replied, "Yes, come."[8] Imagine stepping out of the boat and walking on the water! This all was taking place in the midst of the storm. Not only could Jesus walk on water, but he also made it so that Peter could walk on water. Why wouldn't we want him as our higher power?

Taking your life back will require you to act on what you know about God. You must "get out of the boat" and actually trust him.

Our higher power can restore us to sanity only if we are willing to obey him and keep our eyes on him. (See Peter's downfall at the lake in Matthew 14:30.) James tells us to "get rid of all the filth and evil in your lives, and humbly accept the word God has planted in your hearts, for it has the power to save your souls. But don't just listen to God's word. You must do what it says. Otherwise, you are only fooling yourselves."[9]

Taking your life back will require you to *act* on what you know about God. You must "get out of the boat" and actually trust him.

Our belief in our higher power must eventually translate into faith, trust, and action.

Steps 4–7 and 10: Our Relationship with Ourselves

Once we have an understanding of how we are to relate to God, we look at *ourselves* next. It's time to be honest with ourselves and stop looking at others as the cause of our problems. Step 4 calls for a "fearless moral inventory" by which we examine our own shortcomings and look at how we've been wounded. We look at "sins done by me" and "sins done to me." The apostle Paul writes, "Be honest in your evaluation of yourselves, measuring yourselves by the faith God has given us."[10]

Step 4 has its origin in the four absolutes of the Oxford Group, an early-twentieth-century religious movement: *honesty, purity, unselfishness,* and *love.* Our personal inventory can begin with where we have fallen short on each of the four absolutes. Where, and with whom, have we been dishonest? Where have we been lax in our morality and purity? How have we acted selfishly? And with whom is our ability to love diluted with resentments?

This step is a call to answer Jesus' question, "Why worry about a speck in your friend's eye when you have a log in your own?"[11] In Step 4, we "first get rid of the log in [our] own eye; then [we] will see well enough to deal with the speck in [our] friend's eye."[12] We work on ourselves first.

Some people get stuck at Step 4. A "searching and fearless" inventory of ourselves seems like too big of a task. We've already looked thoroughly at our wounds, and now we have to look at our failures, too? Well, yes. They go together, really. So we have to be thorough. That can easily get us bogged down and out of touch with our lives again. But our inventory doesn't have to be exhaustively complete. It only needs to represent where we are today, with what we can identify today. As we find out more about ourselves—say, at

Step 10—we'll come back and do Steps 4 and 5 again. That's how the process works.

As we take our lives back, we're not only able to be honest with ourselves, but we're also willing to move to Step 5: being honest with God and with another person. This is putting into action what James instructs us to do: "Confess your sins to each other."[13] We will never take our lives back if we balk at this confession. Remember, "you can't heal a wound by saying it's not there."[14]

Step 6 involves a willingness to have God change us and remove our defects and shortcomings. Before God will act, we must be *willing*. Are we ready to have him take these things away? It seems like a simple question, but it isn't. God may want to remove some things that we're not quite ready to let go of. We're not sure we can—or even want to be—honest about *that*! That's why it's a two-Step process: *readiness* and then *humbly asking*.

Are you really ready? It's easy to say that we're ready to surrender something to God, but if we're not really ready, we'll just be trying to take it back a little bit later. The question of readiness is the point at which we begin to face the reality of living differently.

Then we come to Step 7, where we pray and ask God to remove our shortcomings. This is a serious step, and God takes it seriously. We need to be ready for the changes he is going to bring to us. (As we mentioned in our discussion of Step 4, and as Step 10 reminds us, this is not a "once is enough" effort.) Change is an ongoing process. Because we all continue to sin, we must stay current with taking our inventories.

Change is an ongoing process. Because we all continue to sin, we must stay current with taking our inventories.

This process is really *a different way to live*—a more authentic and progressive way to live. But as we go back to Steps 4 and 5 again, this time we know what to do with them, and we have a better understanding of how to keep moving forward. I (David) still take a periodic moral inventory to remain aware of my inner character.

Steps 8 and 9: Our Relationship with Others

When we worked Step 4, we were already starting to work on Step 8. Part of our moral inventory includes the beginnings of our list of people to whom we need to make restitution. It is a form of hypocrisy to pursue a deeper relationship with God when we have human relationships that must be made right. That's why Jesus said, "If you are offering your gift at the altar and there remember that your brother or sister has something against you, leave your gift there in front of the altar. First go and be reconciled to them; then come and offer your gift."[15]

Because Jesus gave this teaching in Galilee, which was a three-day journey from the Temple's location in Jerusalem, those who heard him would have had a vivid picture of the importance that Jesus placed on restitution and making amends.

He was telling his listeners to leave their sacrifice on the Temple altar and make a three-day journey back home, to make amends, and then to travel three days back to Jerusalem to offer their sacrifice. Jesus knows that making amends is difficult,

Making amends is a key to taking our lives back. We must try to make things right with people we have harmed or hurt.

but it is worth every bit of effort! Making amends is a key to taking our lives back. We must try to make things right with people we have harmed or hurt.

Experience has shown that if we postpone action on these two steps, we short-circuit our growth and healing. At Step 3, we surrendered our will and chose to follow God's will. But if we truly want to follow God's will, we will be more than willing to make amends. It's the loving thing to do, as the apostle John reminds us: "Whoever claims to love God yet hates a brother or sister is a liar. For whoever does not love their brother and sister, whom they have seen, cannot love God, whom they have not seen."[16]

Jesus spoke directly to this issue when he said: "If you are even angry with someone, you are subject to judgment! If you call someone an idiot, you are in danger of being brought before the court. And if you curse someone, you are in danger of the fires of hell."[17]

We must approach Step 9, as well as all the other Steps, with prayer and an attitude of humility. Apart from God's leading, how can we know that our going to some people to make amends won't cause them greater harm? Some situations may seem obvious, but there are circumstances we might not be aware of that only a word from God can make clear.

Everyone we've talked with over the years who has completed Steps 8 and 9 has reported how free they felt after following through with someone—even with just one. Think of how free you will feel after you have covered your entire list.

Step 11: Strengthening Our Relationship with God

To highlight that this is a spiritual process, we come back to our relationship with God in Step 11. He acts as the bookends of our healing journey. We encounter him at the beginning when we turn over our wills and our lives to our higher power, Jesus. Now we are faced once again with the reality of our relationship with God—not just in an act of surrender, but in a journey that involves *ongoing* surrender, along with seeking to know God better.

We can increase our conscious awareness of God's activity in our lives by developing a discipline of spending regular time in prayer. Step 11 specifies that we are to pray "only for knowledge of his will for us and the power to carry it out."

The other facet of our spiritual growth is referred to as "meditation." This means not only spending time reading the Bible, but also spending time being quiet and listening for God's voice—based on what you've read in the Bible.

Step 12: Taking the Message to Others

The healing journey is now summed up as a "spiritual awakening." As we have learned how to take our lives back, and as we have been awakened spiritually, we are to share our journey with others. Be careful, though. Sometimes, people want to *start* with this step. When they think they understand the process but want to avoid the work of actually taking their life back, they can be tempted to try to help someone else take back his or her life. Codependent helping fits so easily into our problem behaviors.

There's a reason why this is the last Step. We're not ready to share our journey until we've had our spiritual awakening. The truth we have to impart is what God *has done* for us, not what he *can do* for someone else. Keep it personal—it's about what God has done *for you*!

We believe that *recovery* is a synonym for what the Bible calls *sanctification*. We're all in recovery from the ravages of sin and our sinful nature, and sanctification, discipleship, and Life Recovery are time-tested paths toward developing into who we really are, as God intended us to be. But this is only part of the healing journey. There's more to come.

14

A LIFE TAKEN BACK

To say that it's not easy to take your life back is quite an understatement. It is a long and difficult journey out of the hell of hopelessness into the challenging but manageable realities of living your life fully in the present, possessed by no one but your real self and God. What so many people never seem to realize is that as difficult as recovery can be, it is usually not half as difficult as staying stuck in the old ways of victimhood, struggling just to make it through to the next day. The old ways are a one-way street leading to greater difficulties, with less hope and deeper despair. Taking your life back puts you on a path full of wonder, meaning, and blessings so plentiful that you can't even imagine all that is possible.

Most of us can't even ask God for this, because the magnitude of everything he has for us is so far beyond our comprehension.

But that doesn't mean we can't take giant steps in the direction of discovering God's best for us. And it doesn't mean we can't live each day with anticipation, hope, and promise. Taking your life back puts you squarely on the path of becoming all that God intends for you to be—a holy vessel, yielded to God for use in service of his perfect plan. From the very beginning, we were designed for intimate relationship with God. And as we rediscover our real self and bring our lives back into alignment with our Creator, we find fulfillment, purpose, and meaning in life.

As we rediscover our real self and bring our lives back into alignment with our Creator, we find fulfillment, purpose, and meaning in life.

Mileposts on the Journey

In this chapter, we want to unpack some of the key ingredients of a "taken back" life. We want you to be able to identify that you are either living out God's purpose for your life or that something is missing and needs attention. No one will ever fully arrive in this life. The journey is the goal. Either we will continue to grow, or we will begin to die bit by bit. Of course, unless Christ returns in the meantime, we all will one day die a physical death, but if we can take our lives back, we can live life to the fullest every day until then.

Because we've all had enough of dying bit by bit, here is one last invitation to rediscover your real self and begin to realize all that God has for you. This invitation comes with a picture of what your life can look like when it is fully yours and fully committed to God. The ideas below do not paint a complete picture—to attempt to do so would be to limit God—but they fill in the blanks enough to give you a vision of a life that most people, we think, would be excited to experience. We hope and pray that you are able to catch a glimpse of the possibilities. It will take hard work, patience, perseverance, and perhaps some counseling and encouragement from others. But it is a blueprint for being restored each and every day.

Seeing

For so much of our lives, we have been blinded by others who have wanted to control us and who actually did. We were blinded by their manipulations of the truth: gaslighting the things they wanted us to see and distorting or denying the things they did not want us to see.

We've been blinded by preachers and purveyors of toxic faith offering us superficial treatments for our deepest wounds.[1] We have tried the quick fixes of some teachers that fixed nothing. And we have experienced their shaming when our faith was labeled as weak, and we have borne the blame when the miracle of an instant solution did not show up.

Now we are aware of the defects we possess and the imperfections of others. We are not blindly idealizing others or idolizing ourselves. We see it all and are aware of the options available to us. We are aware of, but no longer available to, the option to sink back into despair, and we are aware of what it takes to stay on course for living in the hands of God. We see our vulnerabilities and how we acquired them. And we know how easy it would be for someone to tap into one of our weaknesses and trigger us back into sickness. But our ability to see makes that regression a very unlikely scenario. We are aware of our triggers and do not blindly walk into them or expose ourselves to them.

The gift of seeing can sometimes feel like more of a burden than a gift because we know we're responsible for what we see.

The gift of seeing can sometimes feel like more of a burden than a gift because we know we're responsible for what we see. When we were blind victims, we were prone to react to someone else's sickness. Now we see the trap, and we know that we can choose the proper response (not reaction). Even if it is the most difficult choice, we know that it's the one that keeps us free.

Surrendering

Resisting, fighting, justifying, rebelling, and all the other things that children and adolescents do have been replaced with the very adult act of surrendering to God. As adults, we can surrender to him because we know that he really loves us and has only our best interests at heart. We boldly surrender by applying what we have seen work in the lives of others. Complying with that impulse transforms into surrender to God, who is the foundation and source of everything that has worked to help people take their lives back. We often move from our initial surrender into a process of turning more and more of our life over to God. At first we don't understand much about God, but as we work and learn and grow, we find that he is more than worthy of our faith, hope, and trust.

Surrender is often viewed as a one-time event, but we have learned that it is a daily exercise that starts every morning when we connect with God and commit our day to him. And then we're challenged to *stay* surrendered all day long. Moment by moment, we must resist the urge to take back control and run our ship onto the rocks.

We surrender our hurts and our sense of entitlement, our slights and our triggers, because when we don't, we find ourselves trapped by our selfish motivations and actions. Surrender frees us from the harsh, delusional, self-centered choices that allow something or someone else to control what only God deserves to control.

We take our lives back by surrendering them all day, every day, to the one who gives us life.

Feeling

For much of our lives, we have been enrolled in a "dullification" program, numbing ourselves with denial, rationalization, minimization, drugs, drink, sex, compulsive habits, pornography—you name it. We've used things and we've used people, and we did it to survive. We learned to suppress our feelings because whenever we expressed an authentic emotion, someone made it seem as if we were out of line, off-kilter, or somehow sick. Before long, the most common emotions we experienced were resignation, hopelessness, and despair.

When we began to recover our ability to feel, we *felt*. As trite and trivial as it may sound, it's true. Coming out of our dullness, our numbness, we started to feel again, and we started to live with those feelings and get along with them. We did not try to project an aura of perfect peace in every situation—not any more than Jesus did. In fact, we found ourselves acting like the real Jesus, who wept at the loss of a friend, swept money changers out of the Temple in anger, and sweated great drops of blood in the garden of Gethsemane—not because he was mildly agitated but because he was experiencing the deepest of sorrows and the bitterest of griefs.

As our feelings reawaken, we find they are manageable. We learn that feelings make us aware of all that is good and wonderful and vibrant in the real world. They also alert us to areas that need our attention. Feelings of guilt lead to godly sorrow, which motivates us to change and make things right. Fear leads us to evaluate our relationship with God so that his perfect love can cast out our fear and we can be rooted and grounded in love, not fear.[2] And our anger reveals our unmet expectations. It points us toward the bitterness that is eating us up and the resentment that is tearing us down. We feel it and we deal with it, and we learn that we are able to survive the feelings that go along with living out of our real self. There's no need to manufacture fake feelings. They never last, never satisfy, and never leave us in a better place.

So we feel all the crummy stuff, and we get through it, but we're also now able to feel more of the glory of God and the wonder he

As our feelings reawaken, we find they are manageable. We learn that feelings make us aware of all that is good and wonderful and vibrant in the real world.

puts before us. The reward for experiencing the horrible feelings is that the experience frees us to be engulfed with joy over the simple blessings of life. Feelings used to be what drove us crazy. Feelings made us miserable. But they also pointed us back toward home, and they will keep us pointed toward our ultimate home if we stay open. We continue to feel, and with each feeling we uncover the source of the emotion and pay attention to what it is trying to reveal to us.

Believing

On our journey to take our lives back, we may have been plagued by doubt as we struggled to make sense of it all. Questions rambled around in our heads about God regarding where he was and what he was up to. *How could a loving God do this to me? How could a loving God allow this to happen to me? Why didn't God prevent this horror? Now that it has happened, why doesn't God fix what he didn't prevent and soothe what he allowed to hurt me?* We doubt, ruminate about our doubt, and leave God out of all the conversations going on inside our heads.

When we started believing, we began to surrender. It was the beginning of a genuine faith that guides us each day as we choose God and God's ways.

God was always there, but because he didn't perform according to our expectations or on our terms, we didn't really believe in him or trust him. Our faith was dead, or at least hindered, because we were unwilling to surrender our will to a God we could not control. But as time moved on and humility crept in, we came to believe that God is real and that he is not required to jump through hoops like a trained dog. (Yes, that sounds flippant, but isn't that, in effect, how we often approach God?) We awoke to the startling reality that we are not alone, and we never have been. We believed.

When we started believing, we began to surrender. It was the beginning of a genuine faith that guides us each day as we choose God and God's ways over a false image of a God who would allow us to play God ourselves. Our belief is no longer in ourselves or our ability to control our lives. Our belief is in a God who has everything under control.

Healing

We know the feelings of stagnation and sickness that accompany a rotting soul. We have maintained and wallowed in the sicknesses of our lives by allowing ourselves to be taken over by someone or something other than God. We have experienced the frustration of not growing because we could not grow under the control of our sick souls. Healing had to come first. Taking our lives back was a healing balm. Even the process of *starting* to take our lives back was healing, though painful. The scalpel of truth, wielded by a wise and loving Holy Spirit on a surrendered and willing heart, did its work on us so that we could heal.

Perhaps the most healing action we took was to open up to someone else about what we had done or allowed to be done to our lives. After looking for and praying for and begging for a breakthrough from God, all it took was a willingness to be honest with someone else and allow him or her to hear the truth about us. That began a healing process that continues today. Though the physical effects of aging are immutable, our healing souls are experiencing the youthfulness of eternity. We are just getting started on a path that will one day result in an ultimate and divine healing of every part of our being. For now, we patiently experience what is in front of us, and we continue to strengthen our lives by allowing God to do for us what we cannot do for ourselves: heal our souls and restore our spirits.

Choosing

There was a time when every decision was made for us by others. As we grew up, we began to make choices of our own. Sadly, that decisiveness did not last. Somewhere along the line, we allowed other people or things to start making choices for us again. We passively complied and turned our lives and wills over to someone who did not have our best interests at heart.

We chose that path until we reached a point of frustration and pain that made us realize we had surrendered our freedom to choose—and we resolved to take that freedom back. We began to break free, to heal, and to surrender our lives to God rather than be controlled by anyone more powerful than we were. Now that we have chosen God, we continue to choose him each day by walking along his path. We are able to stay on that path by deciding to do "the next right thing," even when it is the toughest thing to choose at the moment of decision.

In aligning our wills with God's, we recapture an essential part of our purpose and design, and we rediscover a dream that we may have thought had passed us by.

In aligning our wills with God's, we recapture an essential part of our purpose and design, and we rediscover a dream that we may have thought had passed us by. It is a dream of choosing our own path and destiny in accordance with God's will for us. It is the dream of choosing what is *best* for us rather than what is merely permissible or expedient. It is the dream of living one day at a time, not in the mire of our past or in fear of an unpredictable, uncontrollable, and unknowable future. It is the dream of choosing to live in the most manageable *present* we have ever known.

Searching

As victims, we looked for a way to survive, and we survived. We made it through and made it out, and now we have begun to take back our lives that we once thought were lost forever. A nobler search has now replaced our search for survival. Now we search for truth and wisdom from God that will guide us in all we do. And more and more, that wisdom and truth will come to characterize our lives. We've also become empowered to search for the truth about ourselves. We look for *why* we choose what we choose and *why* we allow what we allow. We search for the feelings behind the feelings we experience each day. We search for truth without distortion or manipulation. We never stop searching for the truth that guides us toward making our story part of God's Kingdom story.

Every day, as we search for truth, for what's best, for God's will, and for God's redemptive purpose for all we've been through, we're searching for wisdom that will make sense of it all. And as we search for and find ways to mend the brokenness that has controlled too much of our lives for too long, we become able to help others in their brokenness. We have found others who need us as much as we need them.

Connecting

Isolation, detachment, and lonely darkness have been eliminated, eradicated, and swept clean from our lives. Anytime we have been tempted to fall back into their discomforting familiarity, we choose instead to connect. We once felt unworthy of connection and feared that rejection would be the outcome. We were told that we were not entitled to connect with God or anyone else. We survived all alone inside our heads and hearts.

Now life is different, as we connect in ways we once thought were impossible. We bond with others out of a true desire to know them and care for them. We also connect because we want to be known and we have nothing to hide. Our connections are mutually beneficial and give us a delightful sense of what it means to be an adult. We love finding new ways to connect more deeply with those who are close to us, and we connect more regularly with those who are not as close.

Connection has turned our painful suffering upside down. We participate actively in groups with people who understand how we have suffered, who know how easy it is to fall back into needless suffering, and who accept us because they know we deserve to be on equal footing with our fellow strugglers. Our connections enrich us as we share with others, hear their stories, and learn from their sources of strength and discoveries of hope. Our past refusal to connect and our unhealthy connections used to be destructive to us. But connecting now brings us life, strength, hope, and the surprising element of reasonable happiness right where we are. We did not find this by withdrawing or moving on. We found it by connecting with other people, often one person at a time.

Connecting now brings us life, strength, hope, and the surprising element of reasonable happiness right where we are.

Belonging

We were outcasts, rejects, and abandoned souls who drifted in darkness under the influence of dark and evil forces. We belonged to no one, yet we allowed outside influences to control us and destroy us. The things we belonged to only hurt us. Now we belong to God. We belong to God's people. We belong to Life Recovery groups. We belong to healthy families, or we create healthy families to help us heal from our sick families of origin.

God set a place at the table for us. We belong to healthy groups of people living out their purpose and being fulfilled as they help and are helped by others. We are no longer an adjunct to someone else's life. We belong. We deserve to show up, and others deserve to have us there. We are included, and we love being part of something far greater than ourselves.

Receiving

There was a time when we gave everything we had to whatever or whoever demanded it. We began our lives with such drive and power, and all of that was stolen from us. We worked hard to please people or meet their demands, and we used ourselves up. Acting under our own power, we ran out of gas.

Now that we have taken our lives back, we have the power we need to live life with purpose and meaning. We feel God's love in intimate times of connection with him, and we feel it in the hugs and handshakes of his people. We are able to receive from others, rather than always trying to produce, perform, or please. Our relationships are mutually beneficial as we speak truth and life to one another. And we experience the joy of pleasing God while receiving his nurturing care.

Now that we have taken our lives back, we have the power we need to live life with purpose and meaning.

Agreeing

Rather than always defending our actions, we are free to agree when we have done something wrong to ourselves or to others. But we no longer agree to live in shame or under the control of another person. We do not agree with things that are untrue merely to keep the peace. We affirm truth and everything that brings life. We are honest about our lives, and when the Holy Spirit pricks our conscience, we agree, confess, and repent from our shortcomings and do what we have to do to correct our defects of character.

We agree with God every day that our lives are a gift from him, and we are committed to live in his truth. When we are tempted to attach half-truths and toxic distortions to our reality, we choose not to. We agree only with what agrees with God, and we are free to admit that we are in alignment with truth.

Reflecting

Whereas our lives were full of busyness and hurry, we now set aside time for quiet reflection. A favorite chair or a sofa or even a comfortable place on the floor provides a spot where we can think about our lives and learn from our experiences.

This new contemplative approach has helped our lives to grow in richness and value because we take time to consider truth, noticing how we have utilized it, how we have veered away from it, and what we need to do differently.

We also reflect on our unmet needs and hopeful desires, and at times we even write down our thoughts to revisit in the future. We have learned to embrace wisdom as we have devoted time for reflection on events, choices, consequences, and accomplishments that we once thought were not possible.

Stabilizing

We don't need storms anymore. We don't need to stir up trouble to prove that we exist or find a momentary spark of conflict to give us energy. We no longer traffic in the extremes. We are clear about who we are and why we are here. We are secure in our relationships with God and with others, and we foster stability in our relationships. The longer we live surrendered to God and the more we incorporate his truth into our daily living, the more stable we become internally, relationally, and spiritually. Every day that we live in harmony with our true self creates even more stability than the day before. We will occasionally miss the excitement of the hurricanes we whipped up in our time of sickness, but we don't miss them enough to threaten or destroy the stability we are creating one day at a time.

Learning

Humility is essential for learning. As we humble ourselves before God, we learn new ways of living, interacting, relating, and becoming the person who God created us to be. We learn from our defective choices, and we learn from those great moments when we choose "the next right thing" and reap the rewards of living beyond our own immediate urges and impulsive drives.

We pursue learning because we want to grow and live with wisdom beyond our years. Learning is a process, and we have come to enjoy the process rather than waiting impatiently for results to materialize. In our relationships, we are learning more and more about healthy boundaries—where we stop and where others start. And we are learning how to prevent ourselves and others from invading spaces we are not entitled to inhabit. We are learning to find the lessons in everyday life and to be grateful for the simplest pleasures and the most complex difficulties. Each day and each situation presents fresh opportunities for learning, and we are learning to be wise—but not to think ourselves so wise that we become fools.

> *Every day that we live in harmony with our true self creates even more stability than the day before.*

Building

We have been torn down and torn apart, and we have done the same to others and to ourselves. When our foundations were weak, it didn't take much to bring destruction. But now we are building in ways that will last for eternity. On the foundations of faith, humility, truth, wisdom, openness, and intimacy with God and others, we are building our lives and helping others build theirs with strength and the wisdom of God's perspective.

There were times when everything was falling apart and coming undone, and all we could do was pick up the pieces and try not to lose any of them. Now we are building something meaningful and worthwhile out of the brokenness of the past. We are building each other up, and we are building our future. We are building every aspect of ourselves—body, mind, and spirit—to endure the tough parts of life and to be enthralled by great moments that we would have overlooked in the past. Building has become the ongoing process of recovering our lives.

Growing

We have come to understand that if we are not growing, we are dying in some way. We choose to grow. Growth requires restraint and self-control. We restrain our impulsive desires even as we feel the discomfort of putting off instant gratification and maintaining control of our lives.

We choose growth because it enriches our lives, expands our perspective, and increases our opportunities to add new dimensions to our lives.

We grow in our relationships with others by putting them first when appropriate and by making our own growth a priority when something would stunt it. We choose growth because it enriches our lives, expands our perspective, and increases our opportunities to add new dimensions to our lives. We choose growth because it is the only way to find true satisfaction in our lives. Doing nothing and going nowhere are no longer options for us.

Integrating

Our job since we were adolescents was to integrate every part of ourselves into healthy, whole, and functioning individuals. Instead, we maintained the "shameful splits," with parts of ourselves split off from the rest. We had a split-off spiritual part that we dressed up for church but never brought home. No one at home or work observed anything spiritual about us. We were just doing what we were taught: fake it and forget it. We had a split-off sexual life filled with lusts and impulses and urges that we entertained in secret even as we were overtaken and controlled by them. We had a split-off compulsive part of ourselves that would eat as if there were no tomorrow. We would hide it, disguise it, and act as if it didn't exist. But when we keep parts of our lives private, secretive, and compartmentalized, it splits us into pieces.

But now that we have taken back the process of maturing, we are integrating all our "parts" so that everything functions in concert with everything else. Our secretive and compulsive behaviors are confessed and repented of; our social life reflects our spiritual values and corresponds with how we treat others at home and at work; and our emotions flow naturally from the integration of everything working together. Integration is so much more enjoyable and sustainable than trying to maintain one identity at work, another identity at church, and yet another identity at home. We're no longer satisfied with any part of ourselves that isn't working consistently and congruently with all the other parts.

Forgiving

The bitterness and resentment we harbored is gone. The lack of forgiveness that held us captive no longer holds us in bondage. We have been forgiven much, and we now freely forgive others. We look inside ourselves to unearth any seeds or roots of bitterness, and we pull them out before they can entangle us in an unhealthy mind-set. Bitter baggage is kicked to the curb. Residual resentment is being cleansed from us daily as we allow God's grace to wash over us. We want to forgive others because we have seen what a waste and a burden

We're no longer satisfied with any part of ourselves that isn't working consistently and congruently with all the other parts.

unforgiveness is in our lives. We deserve better than to be owned by any past event that has hurt us. We're not naive enough to think we can quickly and completely forgive every offense or major hurt. Forgiveness is a continual process, and we continually pursue it. We realize that if we don't forgive others, God will not forgive us.

Resolving

We have caused problems and created conflict as our desire for control overcame our desire to live and let live. So we go back and resolve our issues. We don't leave them unattended or hanging in the air. Wherever we can promote peace, reconciliation, and healing, we do. Where we can bring clarity, we do. When we are wrong, we can ask for forgiveness. When we are misunderstood, we go back to clarify, correct, and seek understanding.

When we are wrong, we can ask for forgiveness. When we are misunderstood, we go back to clarify, correct, and seek understanding.

In the past, we fled from conflict and avoided confrontation. But now we are free and confident in addressing issues. Not everything is a confrontation. We don't always have to be right or look good. We are able to choose humility if that is what is needed to resolve heavy issues of the heart.

Restoring

In the past, we allowed things to be stolen from us—important things, such as our freedom. We don't do that anymore. We have worked on restoring what has been lost. We see what we have lost, and we have asked for God's help in restoring our sanity, our stability, and the sacredness of our souls.

We may also have been part of taking from others—leeching on them, overly depending on them, manipulating them, and caring more about our own needs than theirs. Not anymore. We are now working to give back, replenish, and replace what we have taken. The Lord has restored our souls, and we in turn are working to restore the souls of others. We are a walking restoration ministry because we have felt the power of God's restorative work in our own lives, and we want to share it with others.

Reaching

There was a time when we sat and waited for people to reach out to us, and we became resentful when it didn't happen. But we're no longer sitting around waiting to be validated or noticed. We're busy reaching out to others and attending to their needs. We extend ourselves not only to those we have hurt or those we already know but also to fellow strugglers and strangers. We want to share with them the hope we have discovered, which has made such a difference in our lives. By reaching others, we bring redemptive value to all that we have endured.

When our days of self-obsession ended, our reaching out to others began. Where self-obsession left us empty, reaching out fills us up. Every now and then, we sense that all our pain and suffering was meant to prepare us to help others in their pain and suffering. Not that all our pain was meant to be; after all, God didn't force us to make those selfish decisions. But God has wasted nothing of our suffering, and when people see us reaching out to others, they say that it seems like a calling from God on our lives. In reaching out, we have found new life as others have responded to our love, care, and concern for them.

In reaching out, we have found new life as others have responded to our love, care, and concern for them.

Sharing

In our old mind-set, we felt so deprived that we hoarded everything or held onto it tightly. Anything we acquired we felt compelled to keep forever. Letting something go was like tearing out our heart. We wasted money on things we didn't need, but then we kept them anyway, never considering who else might benefit from them. Sometimes all our junk proved we were alive.

If we didn't hoard junk—for many, that was too obvious—we hoarded our talents and our time. We kept our spiritual gifts to ourselves, hiding the light of God under a bushel.

As we became grateful for all that God has done for us, we became more generous, as well. Our willingness to share blossomed even more as we came to believe that God cared for us and would provide for us. We no longer believed that we must acquire everything through our own might and power. We trusted God enough to let go of the things that were strangling us, and we began to share more freely with others. We discovered the truth that it is more blessed to give than to receive. We now wake up wondering who needs us, or who needs what we have, and what we can do to share God's awesome blessings with others.

Serving

In our old lives, we served like slaves—under compulsion from whoever or whatever controlled us. We became enslaved to our defects and shortcomings, our obsessions and compulsions, as they took over more and more territory in our lives. Or we served ourselves, trying to find new ways to fuel our survival. It was all about us.

We have stepped outside ourselves with acts of service that return to us more than we could ever give.

Now we serve because we feel called by God to do it. We serve from a grateful heart as an act of gratitude. We want to serve others as our Lord has served us. We want to leave a legacy of serving. We choose to serve because it is proof that we have the power and freedom to choose something rewarding rather than something degrading. And we have experienced the joy of being recognized as ones who serve and appear to love doing it. We have stepped outside ourselves with acts of service that return to us more than we could ever give.

Giving

Before we took our lives back, we were takers from others. We took by robbing others of their time, stealing their confidence, or ripping off their reputations. We took all we could from anyone who was vulnerable because we thought we deserved it and no one else did. We were greedy for whatever we could take, but it was never enough to satisfy us.

Now we not only give but give sacrificially. Before, if we gave anything at all, it was out of a surplus we had acquired. Now we don't care how much we have. We care about others. Not in a sick way, as before when we gave on demand or when shamed into it. Now we give because we are generous of heart. We have matured to where we don't need much, and we love to give to those who have nothing or who lack something in an area where we can help. Often, the easiest thing to give is money—which also limits our involvement. But now we go beyond financial giving and also give of our time, attention, and talents to make the lives of others better.

Leading

Perhaps the most amazing evidence that we have taken back our lives is when people see us stand up and lead. When we were not in possession of our lives, our backs were bent and our spirits were decimated. Now we have a newly found confidence that we have something to offer to others. Forged in the crucible of our struggles and past experiences, we hope for elements of wisdom, understanding, and compassion to be evident in our leadership as we reach across to others to encourage them on their journey.

There was a time when we could not even bring ourselves to attend a meeting of fellow strugglers, and now we are willing to lead others in a group. People observe the changes in our lives and want what we have, and we lead them to the truth. We don't need to lecture or scold; we show with our lives that God has something more in mind for all of us than suffering and surviving. Having found a way out of both, we are eager to lead others to the source of this new way of living that has brought so much joy and fulfillment from so much pain and emptiness.

Providing

We are no longer on a path of needing to take what we can from anyone who will give it. We are providers, contributing to God, others, and ourselves. To God we offer honor, gratitude, and adoration. We humbly lift our hands, bow our heads, bend our knees, and raise our voices in praise and worship of the one true God, who brought us out of captivity and who provided the strength we needed to take our lives back. In our gratitude, we provide God with well-deserved celebration and devotion.

We provide time and attention that our friends and family need in order to be nurtured and to grow.

We now recognize that we have the resources to provide for others. We provide time and attention that our friends and family need in order to be nurtured and to grow. We provide them with encouragement, affirmation, and respect when and where it is needed. We have no need to withhold what we can provide. When it is our role or responsibility, we work dependably and provide financial stability to those who rely on us to do so.

We don't neglect to provide for ourselves. We work, if we can, to earn money to live and give. We stop working when we need to, so that we can provide our souls with the necessary rest, reflection, and resources to keep ourselves safe, protected, and healthy. It feels good to have moved beyond needing so much all the time to providing all that we can to ourselves and others. And it feels good to express our gratitude to God, who was there for us and with us in every moment of the suffering and the surviving, even when we didn't feel it.

Utilizing

We have moved beyond fearing to request help or utilize the help that is available. We no longer believe that we must have all the strength and knowledge within ourselves to get better. We utilize

God's strength and the strength that comes in relationships and community with others.

We are aware of, and use, resources that enrich our lives. We read our Bibles, read useful literature, go to meetings, seek counsel, and find guidelines; and we utilize them all. We have moved from recognizing the helpfulness of a resource to actually using it. We are reaping the benefits of being resourceful in all areas of our lives. Our strength increases each day because we apply what we have available in order to become all that we can become.

Comforting

We once were without the comfort of God because we had cut ourselves off from him. Now, having found God's comfort, we want to comfort others with the same comfort that comforted us.[3] Formerly, we were often the victims of another's lack of caring or even cruelty. We survived. We survived and learned and surrendered and watched as God worked with us and transformed us. Now, with hearts of compassion, we are compelled to comfort others.

We also comfort ourselves. We have found good things that encourage us and restore us instead of tearing us down further. We pray, meditate, talk with friends, draw, write, journal, create, have quiet times with God, spend quality time with others, and sometimes do nothing at all. We don't wait to be comforted; we have learned the healthy art of self-comfort, and we take time to receive and experience comfort from God, others, and ourselves.

We have learned the healthy art of self-comfort, and we take time to receive and experience comfort from God, others, and ourselves.

Experiencing

Our lives were once filled with distractions and obsessions. Rarely were we fully present wherever we were. We were either full of

197

anxiety, focused on our past, or fearing the future. We avoided, ran, moved on, and remained disengaged. No more.

Now we experience the joy of being where we are and engaging with others. We don't have to worry about looking back and thinking about what we missed. We are living in the present—enjoying life as it unfolds and experiencing everything as never before. Before, we could not imagine that engaging with others and experiencing life together could provide such fulfillment. Now, we look forward to discovering new ways of experiencing more of life with our loved ones.

Protecting

We value our lives and the progress we've made. We don't want to lose it, so we protect it. We don't go it alone anymore. We gather with others for strength and hope, and to remind ourselves how far we have come. We are not complacent. We consistently pursue healthy and healing attitudes and actions. We protect ourselves with truth—discovering it, learning from it, growing from it, and never wandering from it.

We are quite aware of dangerous places and people, and we don't compromise or expose ourselves needlessly to either one. We have changed where we go and whom we go with, in order to protect the gains we have made. Grounded in reality, we are not confused about our condition or how far we've come. We protect our progress by investing our energy in others who help us stay grounded in reality and in God's truth and power.

We also protect ourselves by having a plan in place for what to do if we stumble, fall back, or completely relapse. We know what we must do to regain lost ground. We protect ourselves from dropping back into old patterns out of guilt and shame by recognizing that relapse is not a failure but rather a learning experience that opens our eyes, gets our attention, and shows us what we still need to do to fully take our life back. It's a reality check that tells us either that we need to do more or we need to do what we're already doing with greater honesty and authenticity.

Eventually, we master the art of self-protection, and our circle widens to protect others. We gently guide them, affirm what they are doing right, and nudge them back onto a healthy path when they need a nudge. We stand *up* for them and stand *in* for them because we choose to, not because of any demand. We are not driven by shame to protect others. Our gratitude for getting our own lives back, recognizing with fresh eyes all that is worth protecting, moves us to protect those who need assistance in taking their lives back. By standing together in faith and love, we rely on God—our shield and our refuge—to hold at bay the forces that would bring us down and back into old ways of life that did not serve us well.[4]

We take protective action because we are worth protecting. We protect others because we see their worth and are no longer trapped by self-obsession.

Persevering

The Bible clearly states that those who persevere will be honored—not for getting through the challenges in perfect order but just for getting through the challenges. James 1:12 says it this way: "God blesses those who patiently endure testing and temptation. Afterward they will receive the crown of life that God has promised to those who love him." On those days when we experience a setback or feel like a failure—and we all have those days—we keep moving forward. When we fall down, we get back up. If we get back up one more time than we fall down, we are doing all that God has asked us to do.

At one point, we were victims of the past, of circumstances, of the cruelty of others, and of our own mistakes—some of which we never would have made had we not been the victim of someone else's abuse, neglect, or cruelty. But now we're in a different place. We're not back in the Garden of Eden. We're still on this side of Eden's fence, and on this side there are weeds and wickedness that can throw us off at every turn. But we do not have to succumb. We have tasted defeat, and we have enjoyed some significant victories. We must not go back to the old ways. We must not stay down when we fall. We must rally our faith (even faith the size of a mustard seed), persevere in prayer, and enlist the help and support of others to keep us moving forward. We learn to persevere through the most difficult times, so we can live to experience all of the blessings God has for us and for those we love.

When we fall down, we get back up. If we get back up one more time than we fall down, we are doing all that God has asked us to do.

One Last Word

When you consider everything that goes into taking our lives back and *living* our taken-back lives, it is quite a wonderful picture. It is a picture of God's faithfulness, power, and grace. It is a picture that is complete and whole and full of purpose and meaning. It is a picture of fulfillment, joy, peace, and even happiness. It is what we want for you. It is what God wants for you. We hope and pray that this book will open your eyes to the possibility and promise that you can experience fullness of life—today, tomorrow, and forever. As we type these last few words, we are praying God's healing and blessings on you. We hope and pray that this little book will be a catalyst as you take back the rich and full life that God intends for you. And may you never give it up again! We leave you with one last encouragement: Stay the course! Trust God. Persevere, no matter what.

Take your life back, and give it all to God!

Notes

CHAPTER 1: THE PRODIGAL ON THE OTHER SIDE OF THE PALACE

1. Philippians 3:19.
2. Benjamin Ivry suggests this view in his review of *The Return of the Prodigal Son* by André Gide: "Gide's prodigal son returns home, not because he regrets his actions, but because he is poor and hungry." Benjamin Ivry, "Returning Home, Somewhat Changed," *Art around Town* (blog), *The New York Sun*, October 5, 2007, http://www .nysun.com/arts/returning-home-somewhat-changed/63996.
3. Luke 15:18-19.
4. Luke 15:24.
5. Matthew 11:28-30.
6. André Gide, *The Return of the Prodigal Son* (Logan, UT: Utah University Press, 1960), 25.
7. Sheila Walsh, "Will We Miss Our Moment in History—Our Chance to Love the Prodigal?" *The Stream*, March 4, 2016, https://stream.org/will-miss-moment-history -chance-love-prodigal.

CHAPTER 2: UNDERSTANDING YOUR WOUNDEDNESS

1. Genesis 1:27.
2. Genesis 2:23.
3. Genesis 2:25.
4. Genesis 3:7.
5. Genesis 3:10.
6. Psalm 139:14.

CHAPTER 3: WHERE DOES IT HURT?

1. Pat Conroy, *The Death of Santini* (New York: Random House, 2013), 38.
2. Ibid..
3. Ibid., 9.

4. Stephen Arterburn and Jack Felton, *Toxic Faith* (Colorado Springs: Shaw Books, 2001), 19.
5. John 1:14, NIV. Italics added.
6. 1 Corinthians 13:4-7.
7. Jeremiah 6:14, TLB.

CHAPTER 5: THE ORIGINS OF REACTIVE LIVING
1. Cindy Hazan and Phillip Shaver, "Romantic Love Conceptualized as an Attachment Process," *Journal of Personality and Social Psychology* 52, no. 3 (1987): 511–524.

CHAPTER 6: SURVIVING BROKEN ATTACHMENTS
1. Jeremiah 6:14, TLB.

CHAPTER 7: SHAME ON ME
1. Adapted from Stephen Arterburn and Connie Neal, *The Emotional Freedom Workbook: Take Control of Your Life and Experience Emotional Strength* (Nashville: Thomas Nelson, 1997), 63.

CHAPTER 9: THE LOSS OF YOUR REAL SELF
1. Charlotte A. Schoenborn, "Exposure to Alcoholism in the Family: United States, 1988," *Advance Data*, no. 205 (1991): 7. See http://www.cdc.gov/nchs/data/ad/ad205.pdf.
2. Bruce H. Lipton, *The Biology of Belief: Unleashing the Power of Consciousness, Matter and Miracles* (Carlsbad, CA: Hay House, 2008).
3. Candace B. Pert, *Molecules of Emotion: The Science behind Mind-Body Medicine* (New York: Scribner, 1997), 268–274.
4. Paul J. Rosch, "Job Stress: America's Leading Adult Health Problem," *USA Magazine*, May 1991.
5. C. S. Lewis, *The Lion, the Witch, and the Wardrobe* (New York: HarperCollins, 2001), 146.

CHAPTER 10: LOSING TOUCH WITH YOUR SOUL
1. See 2 Corinthians 12:9.

CHAPTER 11: TAKING YOUR LIFE BACK
1. Ecclesiastes 4:9-10.
2. Jeremiah 6:16.
3. Acts 3:6. Italics added.

CHAPTER 12: BECOMING A DECIDER, A DEFENDER, AND A DEVELOPER
1. See 1 Corinthians 7:1-5.
2. See 1 Corinthians 10:13.
3. Ibid.

CHAPTER 13: EXPANDING YOUR RECOVERY PLAN
1. Acts 2:44-46.

2. James 5:16.

3. Italics added.

4. John 7:17, NIV.

5. John 18:6.

6. John 18:3.

7. See Matthew 8:23-27; Mark 4:35-41; Luke 8:22-25.

8. Matthew 14:27-29.

9. James 1:21-22.

10. Romans 12:3.

11. Matthew 7:3.

12. Matthew 7:5.

13. James 5:16.

14. Jeremiah 6:14, TLB.

15. Matthew 5:23-24, NIV.

16. 1 John 4:20, NIV.

17. Matthew 5:22.

CHAPTER 14: A LIFE TAKEN BACK

1. Jeremiah 6:14.

2. See 1 John 4:18; Ephesians 3:17.

3. 2 Corinthians 1:4 (author's paraphrase).

4. Psalm 46:1. See also 2 Samuel 22:3, 31, 36; Psalm 18:2, 30; Psalm 91:4; Psalm 144:2; Proverbs 30:5.

About the Authors

Stephen Arterburn, M.Ed., is the founder and chairman of New Life Ministries—the nation's largest faith-based broadcast, counseling, and treatment ministry. He is also the host of the nationally syndicated *New Life Live!* daily radio program, which airs on more than 180 radio stations nationwide, on Sirius XM radio, and on television. Steve is the founder of the Women of Faith conferences, attended by more than 5 million women. A nationally known public speaker, Steve has been featured in national media venues such as *Oprah*, *ABC World News Tonight*, *Good Morning America*, *CNN Live*, the *New York Times*, *USA Today*, *US News & World Report*, and *Rolling Stone*. In August 2000, Steve was inducted into the National Speakers Association's Hall of Fame. A bestselling author, Steve has more than 10 million books in print, including the popular Every Man's Battle series. He is a multiple Gold Medallion–winning author and has been nominated for numerous other writing awards. He is also an award-winning study Bible editor of ten projects, including the *Life Recovery Bible*.

Steve has degrees from Baylor University and the University of North Texas, as well as two honorary doctorates. He resides with his family in Indiana.

David Stoop, Ph.D., is a licensed clinical psychologist in California. He received a master's in theology from Fuller Theological Seminary and a doctorate from the University of Southern California. He is frequently heard as a cohost on the nationally syndicated *New Life Live!* radio and TV program. David is the founder and director of the Center for Family Therapy in Newport Beach, California. He is also an adjunct professor at Fuller Seminary and serves on the executive board of the American Association of Christian Counselors. David is a Gold Medallion–winning author who has written more than thirty books, including *Forgiving What You'll Never Forget* and *Rethink How You Think*. He resides with his wife, Jan, in Newport Beach, and they have three sons and six grandchildren.

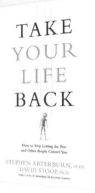
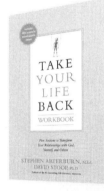
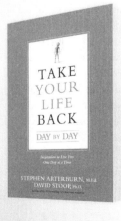

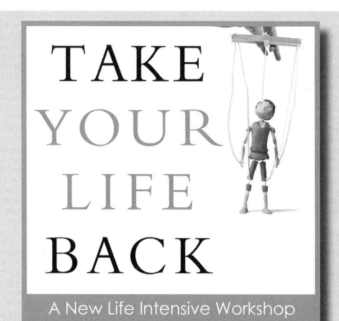

TAKE YOUR LIFE BACK

A New Life Intensive Workshop

Speakers:
Steve Arterburn
and
Dave Stoop

So what's the next right step? Even when you want a life of wholeness, health, and fulfillment, the journey can be filled with painful turns and surprising twists, and it can lead to isolation. But the path toward wholeness is never one you have to walk alone!

Join Steve and Dave at the *Take Your Life Back Intensive Workshop*, where they share more than 8 hours of biblical truths and life-changing information on topics such as "Discovering Who or What Owns You" and "Surviving Broken Connection." A New Life Network Counselor, in small group sessions, will help you process what you have learned and develop a specific and personal plan for your daily life. A plan that, if followed, reveals God's faithfulness in your everyday life, enriches your life and relationships like never before, and gives you the strength and freedom to *Take Your Life Back!*

For information on workshops or to register, call
800-NEW-LIFE (639-5433)
newlife.com

NEWLIFE

CP1154

FIND HEALING IN GOD'S WORD EVERY DAY.

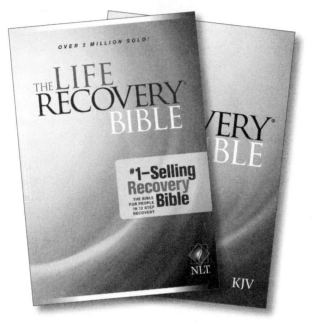

Celebrating over 2 million copies sold!

The Life Recovery Bible is today's bestselling Bible for people in recovery. In the accurate and easy-to-understand New Living Translation, *The Life Recovery Bible* leads people to the true source of healing—God himself. Special features created by two of today's leading recovery experts—David Stoop, Ph.D., and Stephen Arterburn, M.Ed.—include the following:

Recovery Study Notes: Thousands of Recovery-themed notes interspersed throughout the Bible pinpoint passages and thoughts important to recovery.

Twelve Step Devotionals: A reading chain of 84 Bible-based devotionals tied to the Twelve Steps of recovery.

Serenity Prayer Devotionals: Based on the Serenity Prayer, these 29 devotionals are placed next to the verses from which they are drawn.

Recovery Principle Devotionals: Bible-based devotionals, arranged topically, are a guide to key recovery principles.

Find *The Life Recovery Bible* at your local Christian bookstore or wherever books are sold. Learn more at www.LifeRecoveryBible.com.

Available editions:
NLT Hardcover 978-1-4143-0962-0
NLT Softcover 978-1-4143-0961-3
Personal Size Softcover 978-1-4143-1626-0
Large Print Hardcover 978-1-4143-9856-3

Large Print Softcover 978-1-4143-9857-0
KJV Hardcover 978-1-4143-8150-3
KJV Softcover 978-1-4143-8506-8

CP0107